We're in the Money

We're in the Money

Depression America and Its Films

by Andrew Bergman

HARPER COLOPHON BOOKS
Harper & Row, Publishers
New York, Hagerstown, San Francisco, London

A hardcover edition of this book was published in 1971 by New York University Press.

WE'RE IN THE MONEY

Copyright © 1971 by New York University. All rights reserved. Printed in the United States of America. No part of this book may be used or reproduced in any manner without written permission except in the case of brief quotations embodied in critical articles and reviews. For information address Harper & Row, Publishers, Inc., 10 East 53rd Street, New York, N. Y. 10022. Published simultaneously in Canada by Fitzhenry & Whiteside Limited, Toronto.

First HARPER COLOPHON edition published 1972

STANDARD BOOK NUMBER: 06-090270-1

78 79 80   12 11 10 9 8 7

This book is for my parents

Acknowledgments

This book was originally researched and written at the University of Wisconsin as a doctoral dissertation, under the direction of Professor William R. Taylor, now of the State University of New York at Stony Brook. Using movies as documents of the 1930s was an admitted risk; Professor Taylor was never less than total in his commitment to the research, and an invaluable critic.

The staff of the Library of the Performing Arts of the New York Public Library was particularly helpful in connection with unearthing documents for the secondary research. Getting access to the films themselves was less simple, and I must give special thanks to Fred Lugo of MGM, who had prints of a half-dozen films shipped to New York for personal screenings, films not shown in New York for thirty years and films, as it turned out, absolutely vital to the book. The Museum of Modern Art was also extremely helpful in this regard.

A grant from the American Film Institute for 1969–1970 saved the author from languishing on a diet of Saltines in Madison, Wisconsin.

And to my friends—some of whom read parts of this manuscript, some of whom probably never will—thank you for letting it all happen.

Contents

Introduction

For our purposes, Depression America will be a nation of Bijous, Gems, Orpheums, Strands, Rivieras and Mystics. We will concern ourselves with the millions of man-hours spent inside those theatres—the lush, rococo palaces constructed during the 1920s and the drab halls stuck in all the hamlets and farm towns. They were important places during the 1930s.

During the most abysmal days of the early thirties, as economic paralysis spread, snuffing out a shop here, a bank there, a factory somewhere else, movie attendance still averaged an astonishing sixty to seventy-five million persons each week.[1] Although this was a considerable comedown from the one hundred and ten million moviegoers of 1930 (when sound was still a great novelty), it remained a powerful testimonial to the sway movies held over the national imagination. For, as the number of unemployed moved towards fifteen million, and millions more became partially employed, it was evident that the total of sixty million, even counting repeats, included a great many people who could scarcely afford to be there. In those painful days, the marquees of America's

Broadways and Main Streets attracted the dispossessed farmers, the failed bankers and all the sellers who had no buyers.

Americans needed their movies. Moving pictures had come to play too important a role in their lives to be considered just another luxury item. Immediately after the stock market had crashed, motion picture executives began stating that people would part with a great deal before they stopped going to the movies. Harry Warner of Warner Brothers thought that films were "as necessary as any other daily commodities," and E. W. Hammons of Educational Films felt financial hardship would not hurt the industry: people "can always afford the price of a seat . . ." [2] And as the crisis deepened in 1932, Walter Gifford, the head of President Hoover's Organization on Unemployment Relief, advocated the distribution of free movie tickets to the poor. According to Gifford, President of American Telephone and Telegraph, the movies were a necessity to be ranked just behind food and clothing.[3]

The purpose of this study is very simple: to consider what shape this utter necessity assumed during the 1930s. Sixty million persons did not escape into a void each week; escapism is hardly a useful concept. People do not escape into something they cannot relate to.[4] The movies were meaningful because they depicted things lost or things desired. What is "fantastic" in fantasy is an extension of something real. To Arthur Schlesinger, Jr., American film in the thirties had "a vital connection with American emotions—more, I think, than it ever had before. . . . The movies were near the operative center of the nation's consciousness." [5]

As films are not viewed in a void, neither are they created in a void. Every movie is a cultural artifact—deadly as the phrase may sound, associated with pottery shards, stone utensils, and so on—and as such reflects the values, fears, myths, and assumptions of the culture that produces it. As James Agee noted, ". . . every piece of entertainment . . . has nightmarish accuracy as a triple-distilled image of a collective dream, habit or desire." [6] (Nothing so dramatic as a "collective unconscious" is intended; it is simply a matter of the frame of reference the makers of movies work within. And the films produced during the depression years indicate that this frame of reference changed very clearly between 1929 and 1939.)

These are obviously large assumptions. But if the content of American films were merely representative of points of view sprung from the corporate foreheads of Columbia, Metro-Goldwyn-Mayer, 20th Century Fox, Paramount, RKO, United Artists, and Warner Brothers, they would scarcely be worth the trouble of investigation. To justify the assumption that they represent considerably more, some time must be spent on the problem of intent and the relationship between audience, society and filmmaker.

The only study that has attempted to view films as serious reflections of a specific culture is Siegfried Kracauer's examination of Weimar Germany, *From Caligari To Hitler.*[7] Kracauer was attacked, with considerable justification, for his heavy-handed psychologizing and for his loose handling of the "collective mentality." The kinds of assumptions he made, however, are instructive for this study because Kracauer demonstrated how difficult and dangerous it is to draw direct lines between moviemakers and "popular thought."

Kracauer gave two reasons for the fact that "the films of a nation reflect its mentality in a more direct way than other artistic media." One was that movies were produced by a team of creative personalities: "this tends to exclude arbitrary handling of screen material, suppressing individual peculiarities in favor of traits common to many people." [8] On several counts, this is very questionable. Granting Kracauer everything else, ten or fifteen people can scarcely reflect the "collective mentality" of a nation any more than one or two can. By this logic, "spectacle" films (*Ben Hur, The Ten Commandments*), utilizing armies of personnel, are by definition the most central of any culture. Any movie is the result of many individual peculiarities, yet its director and writer remain the welding forces. And those people, unless senile or insane, invariably operate within the social and intellectual sets of their society. They are, simply, time-bound.

Kracauer's second assumption was that motion pictures were meant to satisfy "mass desires." And the film industry, "vitally interested in profit is bound to adjust itself to the change in mental climate." [9] Here he is on firmer ground, yet Kracauer contradicts this assumption in the process of getting entangled with "collective mentality." For Kracauer, films represent "deep layers of collective mentality, which extend more or less below the dimension of consciousness." [10] He reduces his formula of causality to something suspiciously like magic when he introduces this unsupported Jungian premise. The social analyst turns mystic. One critic saw Kracauer assuming that

the writers, producers, directors, actors or technicians individually or collectively "had" an insight about the conflicts taking place in the German soul, without knowing they had it. In some manner, they intuited or otherwise mystically participated in the problems and stresses of the German people. [11]

Kracauer did himself unnecessary damage by leaning so heavily on the belief that moviemakers possessed a mystical insight they could use to play on a national psyche. One can take the perfectly defensible position that in any period of stress (Weimar Germany, Depression America), there are certain tensions which permeate a society and affect the majority of its functioning members, artists and moviemakers included. America's Great Depression was very much a stress period: not since the Civil War had one event reached into so many households and shaped so many destinies. It is a most obvious frame within which to study popular culture.

The premise is not that moviemakers intuited the yearnings of a national unconscious, but rather that they felt the same tensions everyone else did and wanted to represent them in various ways. It is impossible to say with any certainty that a straight line can be drawn from films to popular thought. "Popular thought" is too private, too diverse, too affected by regional differences. But merely taking the intellectual history of the films by themselves provides the richest of sources for studying various of the tensions and assumptions of the period. And the fact of their enormously mass audience guarantees that such a study is not a form of esoterica.

Siegfried Kracauer closed up his last escape hatch when he dismissed the usefulness of box office returns:

> What counts is not so much the statistically measurable popularity of films as the popularity of their pictorial and narrative motifs. Persistent reiteration of these motifs marks them as outward projections of inner urges.[12]

Here Kracauer is true to his mystic design but false to his second premise—that filmmakers, interested in profit, were "bound to adjust . . . to the change of mental climate." The changes in climate, as detected by profit-oriented studios, were reflected at the box office, not by the reception of telepathic waves from the collective unconscious. Kracauer is correct in seeing that mere box office success should not be an ultimate yardstick in gauging the centrality of a given film. Yet it is a fact that some movies are popular and others are not, and when popularity patterns are investigated, there are interesting results.

Why did people flock to gangster films in the early thirties and stop going to Westerns at the same time? What made It Happened One Night, released with little publicity by a second-rank studio, the most enormous success of 1934? And why was Mr. Deeds Goes To Town so beloved in 1936? Why was Duck Soup, now regarded as the ultimate Marx Brothers comedy, the least successful one they made from 1929 to 1937? How does one explain the huge success of the lush musicals in 1933—and their decline in the mid-thirties—or the resurgence of Westerns, along with the "G-Man" pictures, in 1935 and 1936? In all of these questions, box office success by itself is not meaningful. But when it is considered along with socio-political facts of life and the content of the pictures themselves, we have a highly useful tool.

People went to certain kinds of films and cycles began: gangster cycles, "fallen woman" cycles, "shyster" cycles, "backstage" cycles. The cycles emerged and faded over time by a process which the most elementary knowledge of depression conditions indicates was not random. The existence of these cycles, fostered and withered by public interest and disinterest, helps us understand the problem of intent and causality. As Herbert Gans has noted: "The audience is obviously limited by what it is offered, but what is offered to it depends a good deal on what it has accepted previously." [13] The Gans formula is uncomplicated but useful. At given points during the thirties, certain motifs, values, and modes of action were salient, others less so. Thus, one needs no mystical apparatus to perceive that when the state appeared to be helpless, symbols of state and law came off badly in the culture.

What happens in depression movies is that traditional beliefs in the possibilities of individual success are kept alive in the early thirties under various guises, that scapegoats for social dislocation are found and that federal benevolence becomes an implicit and ultimately dead-ended premise by the end of the decade. Hollywood would help the nation's fundamental institutions escape unscathed by attempting to keep alive the myth and wonderful fantasy of a mobile and classless society, by focussing on the endless possibilities for individual success, by turning social evil into personal evil and making the New Deal into a veritable leading man.

Critics of movies in the thirties were sharply divided. Implicit in the reviews of a writer on the left, like Peter Ellis of The New Masses, was the feeling that movies represented the "bread and circuses" arm of a bourgeois ruling clique. From this perspective, movies helped keep the masses hypnotized and off the streets. But sociologist Herbert Blumer, in a 1933 study entitled Movies And Conduct, concluded that the emotions fostered by even the love stories were those "which our conventions and standards seek in some measure to check" and represented "an attack upon the mores of our contemporary life." The emotions raised by Jean Harlow, however, were infinitely less worrisome than those aroused by hard-nosed gangsters like Jimmy Cagney or Edward G. Robinson. Blumer's conclusion, "It is probable that motion pictures exercise this indirect influence upon other phases of our conventional, social and moral order," echoed the feelings of many worried citizens,[14] and eventually resulted in the tough 1934 Production Code. Sex, revenge killing, arson and dynamiting were cut from films. Fears of runaway lawlessness being inspired by Hollywood reflected civic uneasiness over the precarious state of social cohesion. Between *The New Masses* and Blumer lay a considerable distance, yet the possibility for a synthesis seems obvious. One simply states that attacks upon convention presented on the screen stayed in the theatre, that popular anxieties were satisfied, rather than inflamed, by the movies. Having seen the police gunned down in black and white, one felt no necessity to duplicate the deed. Thus the film becomes a socially-conscious circus for the masses. There was that aspect to thirties film, but it is not so simple. The evasions ran deeper, and the myths represented on screen would, in time, become utterly unsupportable. The forms the myths took, and how they changed over time, lie at the very center of the significance of depression movies for America.

A Note on the Movie Industry and the Depression

In 1929, Hollywood was riding the high crest of profits: the introduction of sound had resulted in approximately one hundred million moviegoers per week, a virtual nation.[1] Profits soared: Warner Brothers to seventeen million, Loews, Inc. to nearly twelve million, Fox and RKO to one and a half million.[2] But from 1930 to 1933, the industry saw those profits turn into hefty debits.

That the movie industry suffered during the economic slide should be self-evident, yet Lewis Jacobs' respected history of American film insisted that "for two full years after the stock market crash, the box office had been unaffected, still thriving on the wonder aroused by sound . . . The dangerous year for Hollywood . . . was not 1929 but 1933."[3] Nineteen thirty-three was certainly dangerous, but for Hollywood, as for the entire nation, 1930 through 1932 were hardly less threatening years. And those close to the industry knew it. Hollywood did not dream peacefully through the early thirties, only to be rudely awakened in

1933. If one is to trace any relationship between Depression America and the movies it produced and watched, it seems necessary to point out that, almost from the start, Hollywood observed the economic disaster with great apprehension.

The initial assurances should not be surprising. Carl Laemmle, President of Universal Films, stated in November of 1929 that movie theatres "are the last to feel the pinch and the first to get over it," and Harry Warner and E. W. Hammons avowed the utter necessity of movie-going. Paramount's Adolph Zukor, recollecting in tranquility, remembered that the crash "at first did not affect the motion industry" but was aware of the "hazardous nature" of the picture business and did not expect "complete escape from the ills besetting others." [4]

1930 saw worries begin to nag. John W. Ailcoate, publisher of the trade paper *Film Daily*, summed up the year as "trying and irritating" and underscored "the fact that the survival of this business rests on a continued flow of good products." [5] Cecil B. DeMille clung to Herbert Spencer and saw "uninterrupted prosperity" as a "national disaster":

The year 1931 in the film industry, as was the case with latter months of 1930, will continue to be a test of courage. . . . Artists who can only stand pleasant times and pleasant words are not of lasting value. This year will be a splendid year for the industry, for during it we will see much of the purging effect of that greatest of all natural laws: the survival of the fittest.[6]

The weakest started wilting in the jungle as 1931 opened. Studio jobs which normally opened up after Christmas remained vacant in January, 1931, as New York-based studio executives ordered a "rigid economy wave." [7] Movie theatres began cutting admission prices, by up to twenty-five cents, in an attempt to bolster sagging patronage. By year's end, *The Film Daily Year Book* called the twelve-month period "the most trying year in the short history of screen entertainment." Innovations like increased use of color and wide screen techniques were put aside, and "the last half of 1931 was filled with rumor, uncertainty and turmoil." [8]

And red ink. RKO saw a 1930 surplus of 3.3 million turn into a 5.6 million deficit in 1931; Fox suffered a loss of 5.5 million after a 9.2 million profit the year before; Warner Brothers went from profits of 17.2 million in 1929 and 7.0 million in 1930 to a loss of 7.9 million.[9] Nineteen thirty-one, not 1933, represented Hollywood's first deeply jolting confrontation with the hard facts of America's dying economy; the dream factory was stricken along with the steel factory. Paramount told *Saturday Evening Post* readers to stop worrying: "There's a Paramount Picture probably around the corner. See it and you'll be out of yourself, living someone else's life. . . . You'll find a new viewpoint. And tomorrow you'll work. . . . not merely worry." [10]

Paramount's Jesse Lasky summed up 1931 by recognizing that Americans were "weary and depression-ridden." Only "new ideas" could get people back to the movie habit.[11] Yet Hollywood would suffer badly until mid-1933, and 1932 would be the worst.

The industry's financial downfall could be traced, in part, to its wild and overoptimistic expansion in the mid and late 1920s. The five major film companies of the period (Loews, Inc., Fox, Paramount, RKO, and Warners) fought for control of the country's movie theatres. As their frantic buying accelerated, their "fixed-charge obligations" (the hard cash committed to the operation of the theatres) more than tripled, to 410 million dollars. When the movie public began to stay home, the direct financial impact on movie companies owning theatres was immediate and immense.[12] The movie companies tried to return movie houses to local ownership in 1932, but receipts tumbled further.

John Alicoate's Introduction to the 1933 edition of *The Film Daily Year Book* was free of the conditional optimism of earlier depression prognoses. It reflected the culmination of two years of suffering for Hollywood:

1932 was a trying year for the industry and its close found the fortunes of the business at their lowest ebb. The year marked the end of the so-called era of extravagance. . . . It saw the start of a movement of disintegration culminating in the receivership of Paramount and RKO. . . . Unless the general economic situation takes a decided change for the better, the industry can hope for little in the way of progress and genuine prosperity.[13]

(Adolph Zukor, however, foresaw only that if "general conditions improve or stay at the present level, we will take care of ourselves.") [14] But if they deteriorated? As Roosevelt took office in March of 1933, receipts hit rock bottom: they were forty percent of what they had been in January of 1931.

But by the fall of 1933, the bank scare was over and the industry began slowly to recover. The *Motion Picture Herald* reported that "abandonment of the industry's emergency salary order got underway this week and grosses at motion picture theatres continued improving." [15] Attendance increased and spokesmen felt it "not unlikely that most major companies will show a profit for the first six months of 1934." By the end of 1933, all the big studios reported improvement.[16] Yet the automatic movie-going of the late 1920s was no more; theatre managers had to work for their patronage. And so it was that Bank Night spread across the land. Cutting ticket prices was not sufficient; gimmickry was called for. Charles Urban Yeagar, an official of Fox Theatres in the West, first introduced Bank Night to Colorado. Simplicity itself, Bank Night involved drawing lucky numbers with cash rewards to the chosen few. In a year when people were grateful for the most trifling windfall, it proved an immense success. (Yeagar quit his job with Fox, placed a copyright on the idea, and formed Affiliated Enterprises, Inc. Anyone who wanted to run a Bank Night thereafter would have to purchase a franchise from Yeagar. The depression made him a wealthy man.) [17]

Other gimmicks were devised: Screeno was introduced, and crockery was distributed in lobbies on given nights. Generations of children broke bread over Rialto chinaware. A Brooklyn theatre owner seriously proposed dropping movies from the program: "All we need is [sic] Bank Nights." [18] The gimmicks did help, and during the partial recovery of 1935 and 1936 attendance rose to weekly averages of seventy-five and ninety million. The 1935 edition of *The Film Daily Year Book* saw an "about face on prosperity road" and noted that "competition was never more keen." In the summer of 1936, it was reported that all major companies were running in the black for the first time since 1931.[19] Warner Brothers and RKO were recovering, and the Frank Capra films (*It Happened*

One Night, Mr. Deeds Goes To Town) were starting to elevate Columbia Pictures to the class of a major studio.

The recession of 1937 also hurt Hollywood, but the industry was on a sounder footing by that time. Calamity had been avoided, theatre ownership cut back, and employment in the industry was nearing normal.

But Hollywood had been hurt and deeply frightened during 1930–1933. And the most compelling evidence of its fears lies not in financial reports or the statements of industry leaders; it lies in the films themselves. The preliminaries completed, we proceed to the black and white footage itself.

Part One   1930-1933

1

The Gangsters

<u>Little Caesar</u> wasted no time. The credits ("those who live by the sword are doomed to perish by the sword") and a solitary filling station appeared on the screen. Nighttime. A car pulled in, someone got out of the car and went into the station and the lights went out. Shots. The car tore away. It was a declaration of the gritty realism which would characterize so much of Hollywood's product during the early years of the Depression. After the great box office success of *Little Caesar*, some fifty gang films came to the screen in 1931,[1] causing consternation among civic pressure groups. Theatres were pressured; parent groups and editorials denounced the poisonous effects of gangster heroes on the young.

Will Hays, once chairman of the Republican National Committee and Warren Harding's Postmaster General, was, at this time, President of the Motion Picture Producers and Distributors of America, an industry group which had chosen Hays to help "clean up" suggestive films during the 1920s. Hays responded to concern over gang films by warning that "to over-emphasize the gangster's role in American life is undesirable." Chicago's censor board reported that nearly half the cuts it made in films between 1930 and 1931 were for "showing disrespect for law enforcement" and for "glorification of the gangster or outlaw." One quarter of the New York censors' cuts involved gangster pictures.[2]

The outcry was vocal all through the early thirties. Representative Wright Patman, Texas Democrat, attempted to establish a Federal Motion Picture Commission and claimed that no less than two thousand civic, fraternal, and church groups had asked for federal censorship. The youth of America, Mrs. Robbins Gilman of the national Parent-Teachers Association told Patman's Interstate Commerce subcommittee, were concluding that "law enforcement has no place in our social order." [3]

The Commonweal declared that movies produced a "social milieu that serves as a very fair kindergarten of crime," and *The Nation* accused Hollywood of crowning the lawless "with the Romantic halo of bravery and adventure that helps to disguise their fundamental moronism." [4] When Carl Laemmle of Universal Pictures observed that American newspapers, with their daily helpings of rape and homicide, were at least equal contributors to the unsettling atmosphere, Columbia University's Professor Walter Pitkin produced a blistering reply. Quoting some bizarre "scientific" evidence, Pitkin predicted that when "we can measure psychic intensities . . . more precisely, we shall find that the picture version [of an underworld event] is even 1,000,000,000 times more effective than the printed." Movies, "merely as a form of communication," were "10 to 100 times more effective per unit of time" than printed matter. Weighing psychic intensities against time units, this combination of Marshall McLuhan and Dr. Strangelove confidently labelled gang pictures "the quintessence of degeneration and social poison." [5]

There was action as well as rhetoric. In New Jersey, little Harold Gamble, aged twelve, returned from seeing MGM's gangland film *The Secret Six* and demonstrated what he had learned by shooting a playmate through the head. The result was a ban on gangster films in West Orange and a Chamber of Commerce drive to get them banned entirely from New Jersey screens.[6] But most intriguing was the MPPDA's 1930 Production Code (not enforced with vigor until 1934) which led off with a lengthy and frightened attack on movie lawlessness.

The concern with law and violence was not new. In 1927, the West Coast Association of the MPPDA had agreed to eleven "don'ts" of movie production. Most concerned sex and nudity, with a miscegenation clause thrown in as well. Only one, banning depiction of "the illegal traffic in drugs," touched on the law. By contrast, the 1930 code, formulated in reaction to the first silent gangster films of the late 1920s, such as *Underworld* and *The Docks Of New York*, was obsessed with both the idea and techniques of lawlessness.[7]

(I) Crime Against The Law. These shall never be presented in such a way as to throw sympathy with the crime as against law and justice or to inspire others with a desire for imitation.
  (1) Murder
    (a) The technique of murder must be presented in a way that will not inspire imitation.
    (b) Brutal killings are not to be presented in detail.
    (c) Revenge *in modern times* [my italics] shall not be justified.
  (2) Methods of crime should not be explicitly presented
    (a) Theft, robbery, safecracking, and dynamiting of trains, mines, buildings, etc., should not be detailed in method.
    (b) Arson must be subject to the same safeguards.
    (c) The use of firearms should be restricted to essentials.
    (d) Methods of smuggling should not be presented.

Despite all the clamor and warnings, the simple fact was that a great many people, and not just the young, were going to see the gangsters. And the Code's concern with moviegoers' learning rudiments of dynamiting and perceiving revenge in contemporary application reveals the edgiest aspects of national concern with gangsters.

The box office reception of *Little Caesar* [8] could only increase anxiety among civic leaders, but the combination of moral outrage and financial success had an intriguing effect upon moviemakers. Knowing from box office results that the gang mode was good business, they stepped up production of successors to *Caesar*; aware of their obligations to society, they attempted to rationalize their content.

Thus Will Hays, in his 1932 MPPDA President's *Report*, insisted that "the insistent message 'Crime does not pay,' as flashed from the screen is the most forceful proof of the successs of self-regulation in the motion picture industry." Despite this seeming assurance, he broke down and admitted that "a continued cycle of such themes . . . was not in the interest of the widest possible entertainment program." [9] And Warner Brothers, in a press sheet aimed at exhibitors, gave noticeably strident and nervous advice regarding the exploitation of *Little Caesar*. The tone of Warner's publicists indicated not only their awareness of civic pressures, but an uncertainty over what *Caesar* was ultimately about.

Little Caesar, while it depicts the graphic and hair-raising episodes in the lives of the members of gangland, does not in any way glorify the gangsters. All your campaign should be geared to the theme of the picture. Do not in any way attempt to glorify the gangster or racketeer. In fact it would be well to stress the helplessness of gangland to the law. Follow the ad copy and illustrations in this press sheet to the letter and you will be on the safe side.[10]

Warner's quavering affirmation of the law perhaps best sets the scene for a discussion of the gangster films. It was a jittery society that felt compelled to denounce, and filled theatres to watch, outlaw protagonists.

Little Caesar (Warner Brothers, 1930. Director, Mervyn Leroy)
The Public Enemy (Warner Brothers, 1931. Director, William Wellman)
The classic gangster film was less a barometer of despair than an act of faith. Despite all the gunplay, mayhem, and omnipresence of death, the gangster film of the early thirties served primarily as a success story. That Americans were attracted to outlaws during the Depression's most wrenching years is an undeniable and useful fact, but the manner in which the outlaws operated only reinforced some of the country's most cherished myths about

individual success. The outlaw cycle represented not so much a mass desertion of the law as a clinging to past forms of achievement. That only gangsters could make upward mobility believable tells much about how legitimate institutions had failed—but that mobility was still at the core of what Americans held to be the American dream. Both the bleakness and determined faith of the early thirties are illumined.

Little Caesar, the first great gangster talkie (and, according to young Dwight MacDonald's 1933 judgment, "the most successful talkie that has yet been made in this country" [11]) was what could be called a success tragedy. Caesar Enrico Bandello (Edward G. Robinson) was a figure who followed all the rules of the success model perfected during the late nineteenth century, soared to the top, and was killed. Snaking through a world of diners, alleys, and "Eat" signs to the Big Time of spats, testimonial dinners, and control of the North Side, Rico was a dynamic and tragic figure.

Finding a parallel in history is easy. Read Andrew Carnegie's "The Road To Business Success, An Address To Young Men" and you have the scenario for Caesar. Carnegie's success formula, presented in any other form in late 1930, would have seemed the worst of jokes. Followed by an ambitious and trigger-happy hoodlum, it made perfect sense. As Carnegie said,

It is well that young men should begin at the beginning and occupy the most subordinate positions.[12]

Rico begins very much at the beginning. He and his sidekick Joe Masara (Douglas Fairbanks, Jr.) pull the gas station job described earlier and retire to a local diner. The youthful mobster rankles at his subordinate position: "We're nobodies." Opening a paper over his java, he reads of a Chicago banquet for gang chieftain Diamond Pete Montana and aches with ambition. ("Aim high," said Carnegie. "Say each to yourself, 'My place is at the top.'") "Be somebody," Rico says to Joe. "That's important." Rico walks out of the diner and goes to Chicago. He joins the Sam Vettori mob. Vettori sizes him up: "Little Caesar, eh." "Yeah," says Little Caesar. Again, Carnegie:

. . . live pure respectable lives, free from pernicious or equivocal associations with one sex or the other. . . . The destroyer of young men
is the drinking of liquor.[13]

Rico really does live that pure life as a member of the mob. He
kills and robs, but that must be accepted as given, as professional-
ism, in order to understand what a success story *Caesar* is. "In the
light of his milieu," said Edward G. Robinson of Rico, "and perhaps even in our light, he was kind, generous and on the level." [14]

True to Carnegie's wishes, Rico refuses to drink until the very
end—but his taking to the bottle is the result of his downfall, rather
than a cause of it. (So pure, in fact, is Rico's life style that his drinking is used to gauge the distance he has fallen.) Repeatedly throughout the film, Rico politely declines to tipple. When he is given a
testimonial dinner after rising to the top of the Vettori gang, he
admonishes the reveling thugs in what is nearly a verbatim gangster
translation of Carnegie's advice: "I wish you guys wouldn't get
drunk and raise Cain. That's the way a lot of birds get bumped off."
From the destroyer of young men to the bumper-off of birds was a
distance of setting, not meaning.

And Rico stays away from the girls. This is emphasized in that
same banquet scene. In the W. R. Burnett novel, *Little Caesar*,
Rico arrived at his testimonial with a floozy named Blondy Belle.
Mervyn Leroy had Rico arrive very much alone; inserted in his lines
(otherwise verbatim from the novel) was an embarrassed greeting
of "It's good to see you mugs with your molls." Burnett's Rico mis-
trusted women and feared their ability "to relax a man, to make
him soft and slack." Yet he was given to "short bursts of lust." [15]
The film denied him short bursts of anything save gunfire. Given
Hollywood's tendency, before the enforcement of the Code in
1934, to play up sex, Rico's celibacy is underscored. Women are
a way of getting sidetracked in the pursuit of success. As Carnegie
told the assembled young men of Curry Commercial College of
Pittsburgh in June of 1885: "And here is the prime condition for
success, the great secret: concentrate your energy, thought and
capital exclusively upon the business in which you are engaged."
As W. R. Burnett described the same process: "Rico's great

strength lay in his singlemindedness, his energy and his self-discipline." [16]

For a young man of such high qualities, programmed by Carnegie's God for all the good things in society, 1930 offered few options. By the time *Caesar* was made, and even more surely by the time it was released, the bottom had fallen out. When *Caesar* was released nationally in January of 1931, the total jobless stood at eight million.

Unloosed in the 1870s, Rico could have cornered wheat, built railroads, cheated farmers on freight rates, paid off legislators, and thus achieved a legitimate success. *Little Caesar* was a very old story in America. Rico's nation demanded achievement, wanted it accomplished individually, and, in 1930, lacked the lawful means to bring it off. So it turned to Rico to go through the paces. He proceeded by the following steps:

A. "The rising man must do something exceptional, and beyond the range of his special department. HE MUST ATTRACT ATTENTION." [17] (Rico attracts attention by going beyond his special department of triggerman. He alertly notes a flaw in boss Vettori's plans for the robbery of a night club. The move demonstrates to the rest of the gang that Rico is a planner, a thinker. Vettori doesn't like it.)

B. "Always break orders to save owners. There never was a great character who did not smash the routine regulations and make new ones for himself." [18] (Instructed by Vettori to hold his fire during the night club heist, Rico not only disobeys but shoots no less than a newly appointed Crime Commissioner. The risk is great, but the success of the job is assured.)

C. "Boss your boss just as soon as you can; try it on early. There is nothing he will like so well if he is the right kind of boss; if he is not, he is not the man for you to remain with—leave him whenever you can." [19] (The logic of the gang films was more severe than that of Carnegie. If the boss is not right, get rid of him. When Rico bosses Vettori about a new split of the take, Sam gets shaky and is easily overthrown by Rico. He becomes the boss.)

Rico extends the gang's sphere of influence, attracts attention as an alert entrepreneur and is tapped by the Boss of Chicago (the Big Boy) to succeed Diamond Pete Montana himself as chieftain of the North Side. Having resisted temptation, broken the rules, bossed the boss and shown his eager industry, Rico gets the promised reward: he is practically on top. (And with further plans: "The Big Boy ain't all he used to be neither," he tells Joe Masara.)

Carnegie was silent about what one should do after reaching the summit, but there was a convention and solution in the gangster films: one was killed. It is this logic which turns a success story into a tragedy. Having carried out the master's blueprint to the letter, but having done so outside the law, Rico just has to be killed. Robert Warshow's remarkable essay on gangster movies spoke of this:

No convention of the gangster film is more strongly established than this: it is dangerous to be alone. And yet the very conditions of success make it impossible not to be alone, for success is always the establishment of *individual* preeminence that must be imposed on others, in whom it automatically arouses hatred. . . . The gangster's whole life is an effort to assert himself as an individual . . . and he always dies *because* he is an individual.[20]

Carnegie's model young entrepreneur did not die at the moment of his success; he became, one supposes, Carnegie—running his business and his philanthropy, an honor to his country and to free enterprise. The tragedy of *Caesar* was that a success story inside the law was unthinkable—the only credible success saga was one that ended in death.

Rico's fall is pathetic. Tracked down by police, hiding in flophouses, drinking and whining, his fall is complete and dramatic. When he gets shot down behind a billboard, the camera draws back to reveal that the billboard heralds the star ballroom dancing act of his old sidekick Joe Masara.

The lawful alternative hardly seems real. In the most vibrant of gang films, it never did, certainly not in *The Public Enemy*. Again, alternatives either do not exist at all or are simply laughable. Two brothers come to manhood in a tough Irish neighborhood:

one stays straight, fights in the World War, and returns to his job as a trolley conductor. The other, James Cagney, shoots and fast-talks his way up through the gang world—very popular, a big success. With enough ingenuity, pluck, and street-urchin wit to keep a dozen Alger heroes going, Cagney's Tommy Powers demonstrated again who the heroes really were and where the action lay. But since *The Public Enemy* was produced at a time when public protests against gangster heroes were increasing, the studio made a weak attempt to explain away Tommy Powers' obvious vibrancy. A foreword gravely announced the purpose of the film: "to depict an environment, rather than glorify the criminal."

The sociological deadpan was shattered the moment Cagney strolled across the screen. He was irresistible. In 1932, Lincoln Kirstein (apparently forgetting Alfred E. Smith) called Cagney "the first definitely metropolitan figure to become national."

When Cagney gets down off a truck, or deals a hand at cards, or curses, or slaps his girl, or even when he affords himself and her the mockery of sweetness, he is, for the time being, the American hero, whom ordinary men and boys recognize as themselves. . . . Cagney is not a man, but neither is he a juvenile.[21]

Cagney's jauntiness and insolence, his wise-guy wit and way of opening his mouth a fraction of a second before speaking, made any attempt at deglorification impossible. The opening minutes of *The Public Enemy*, however, plodded through an attempt to "depict the environment" that produced a Tommy Powers. That "environment" laid a heavy causal burden on saloons and buckets of beer. It seemed more like turn-of-the-century joviality than a guaranteed breeding ground for criminality. Far more foreboding was the opening diner of *Little Caesar*, with all the ominous associations of the nighttime roadside hash house. (In thirties film, *Caesar, The Petrified Forest, I Am A Fugitive From A Chain Gang*, in the painting of Edward Hopper, in Ernest Hemingway's "The Killers," the nighttime diner got established as the stopping post for all the outriders of American society.)

When we first see Tommy Powers, aged six, he is being chased by a policeman, and thus we assume that he has been an outlaw since birth. Or are we to assume that x number of local dives automatically creates criminality? Since Tommy's older brother is a model youth, this does not seem to make any sense, unless Mom's influence with the elder is so overpowering that bad outside influences cannot touch him. The "environmental" incoherence was obvious; the film quickly dropped the subject and went on to the good stuff. The reasons for lawlessness must have been self-evident to people in 1931, and *The Public Enemy* could scarcely imagine an alternative to gangsterism, much less dissect the environment that produced it. By 1937, with the very worst of the Depression traversed and the government nearly deified in film, gangsterism had been wrapped up as a "social ill"; *Dead End* would attempt to grapple with slum life. But in 1931 crime was too closely tied to success to be anything but a life style.

So Tommy is a criminal at six and stays that way. A more appealing figure than Rico, Tommy's industrious nature is tempered by an easy acceptance of women (Mae Clarke, Jean Harlow) and liquor. He advances through hard work and ingenuity, but lacks the puritanical fervor of Rico. Cagney's totally engaging man-boy quality made him the resilient figure of the streets, well-equipped for survival. He was the wise kid growing old but still knowing all the answers. When his saintly older brother returns from the war and accuses Tommy of murder, the retort is savage and to the point: "You didn't get those medals holding hands with Germans." When his girlfriend starts to nag, she is rewarded with a face full of grapefruit—a much loved moment in film.

Of course Tommy must die, upon reaching the limousine, custom-tailored stage of gangland notoriety. But his options make no more sense than Joe Masara's ballroom dancing act. Tommy's brother works on the trolley at the film's opening; at its conclusion he is still there, working his way through night school. In 1931, he was lucky to be still punching tickets. While Tommy blazes toward a certain death, his brother wanders in and out of *The Public Enemy*, giving solemn warnings against breaking Mother's heart. When Tommy offers his mother a wad of money, his brother will not let her accept it. She seems unhappy about it all, and Tommy's brother seems like a sap, noble in poverty. As Tommy jeers early in the film, going to school means "learning how to be poor." The insight is perfect: Tommy accepts death more easily than he accepts the life of a drone. Even if his end is to be dumped lifeless into the family living room, swathed in bandages, Tommy's life has had an agenda, has been restless and full of zest. It is what made both him and Rico so attractive to moviegoers. In 1931, one did not go to movies to see trolley conductors working their way through night school. Attitudes toward the law had something to do with that.

THE PARALYSIS OF LAW

City Streets (Paramount, 1931. Director, Rouben Mamoulian)
Corsair (United Artists, 1931. Director, Roland West)
The Secret Six (MGM, 1932. Director, George Hill)

What was reinforcing and affirmative about the gang films was their faith in a beloved, if delusory, success formula. What was negative and despairing surfaced in their treatment of the law. A viable state commands a viable law, and the law depicted, at its best, was never more than something to beat. At its worst, it scarcely seemed to exist. That law and state were inseparable in films of the thirties became especially clear in 1935 and 1936, when the "G-Man" cycle tied an energetic and attractive law to the federal government. Actors like Cagney and Robinson played federal lawmen (see Chapter 7) with the same elan and dynamism they showed as thugs. But exciting and benevolent law was in the hands of the U.S. Government and in fact *was* the U.S. Government. The cop on the beat never really made it, probably because early thirties film made him into such a feckless character. In film after film, in *Caesar, City Streets,* and *The Secret Six,* the police are dreary operatives, slow-talking and vengeful, obvious heavies. Sometimes they never appear at all. A review of *The Public Enemy* observed the absence of a "war between the underworld and the upperworld. Instead, the war is one of gangsters among themselves." [22] The law had little connection to a success game being played outside the facts of national life.

The gangsters kill their own in *Public Enemy* and *City Streets*, a fact that disturbed officialdom, which perceived where this left the law. Thus, when New York's censor board viewed Howard Hawks' *Scarface*, it demanded that the protagonist be captured by police and hung by the law, rather than be rubbed out by his own. It asked also that the title be changed—to *Shame Of A Nation*.[23]

But it made far more sense for the gangsters to do it themselves —it was their world. The police arrived as emissaries of another world. Trailing seconds behind the stock siren sound (a bleak dull noise, a Fate, which droned through many early thirties films), they walk into *Caesar* or *City Streets* as delegates of a paralyzed state. In *City Streets*, they jail Sylvia Sidney, daughter of a top mobster, and sullenly and futilely try to bully her into singing on the old man. The police march into *The Secret Six*, trade "Oh yeah's" with gangster Wallace Beery and then vanish from the film, appearing again only under the command of a masked "secret six," civic leaders suspending due process in the name of crime-fighting.

So insufferable are the police that *City Streets'* hero, Gary Cooper, when asked to join the beer rackets, says "Beer? I'd as soon be a cop as that." The worst of comparisons in 1931: a flat-foot. Coming from Cooper, it was noteworthy, for he was the ultimate lawman in the classic western, *The Virginian*, made in 1929. For the Virginian, law was a righteous code so strict that one hung one's best friend for cattle rustling. Law was civilization— "making new states out of raw prairie land."

But the law of 1931 was not new states, or "a place to raise a family"; it was the copper, the flatfoot, something to duck down alleys from, a knock at the door, a siren. In American film, cop law and cowboy law have alternated as images: law as civilization and decency, law as a club on the head. In the mid-thirties, Cooper would be out west again, in *The Plainsman*, when westerns returned to favor, simultaneously with the coming of the "G-Man" films. G-Man and cowboy served a watchful but benevolent government—law was a positive tool. But in the early thirties, the law seemed stifling and immovable and more than that, a Fate. If the vitality of the law spoke to the vitality of the state, then the evolution of cowboy law from cop law in the 1930s is suggestive. Hoover emerges as a cop, Roosevelt as G-Man and cowboy: crime-stopper and tamer of the beast. The government as grim watchman—slow-moving and cracking the skulls of Bonus Marchers—embraced cop law. An expansive government which identified its actions with the advance of civilization yet did not stray beyond a strict code—this was the law of the cowboy.

The law of the gang films demonstrated the bleakness of the governmental image. When crime was "stopped" in *The Secret Six*, the means utilized were unconstitutional. Masked civic leaders step in to halt the urban hoods, suspend bail for top mobsters and ignore due process. It was a short step from here to the national police of *Gabriel Over The White House*, a bizarre product of William Randolph Hearst's Cosmopolitan studios. Both films showed a marked tendency to suspend quibbling over means and get to the ends, an impatience not so surprising in 1932 and 1933. Without such desperate ploys, the law was a zero. "I think," star Wallace Beery said in a *Secret Six* press handout, "the picture's a darned good idea for a lot of cities." [24] Only by going beyond the law themselves could police shore up their image.

With the law paralyzed and individual success dreams rampant, *Corsair*, however grotesque, is really the ultimate funhouse mirror reflection of American success myths. It was 1931's equivalent to *The Graduate* (1967), questioning the possibilities for work after college. If the graduate of 1967 seemed helpless to relate his experience to meaningful work, the hero of 1931 still had the Carnegie formula to live up to and lacked only legitimate means to test it out. So *Corsair's* Chester Morris, an All-American football hero, becomes a pirate in order to convince his sweetheart that he's "as good a businessman" as her stock-broking father is. He takes a pirate ship a hundred miles off-shore, beyond legal restrictions: the law ceases to exist. It was the purest example of the early thirties' dilemma: how to become a success in a void. A pirate in limbo, the law nonexistent, Morris discovers that "it doesn't matter how you make your money, it's how much you have when you quit." A *Corsair* press release is helpful:

Many All-Americans are faced with the choice between poverty and marrying a millionaire's daughter. Chester Morris is confronted with the choice. But the hero of *Corsair* refuses to play the game that way. He refuses to play the game as Wall Street plays it. He wants a million dollars, but he wants it on his own terms.[25]

In 1931, "his own terms" meant piracy. His girl friend's father is impressed with Chester's initiative. Fittingly, he appoints him president of a South American oil company.

*   *   *   *   *

The years between 1930 and 1932 were the springtime of the American gangster movie. In 1931, the antigangster crusade gained momentum, and by 1932 fewer such films were produced.[26] Censors and civic groups did the job, but the success drive contained in the gang films had no place to go. It reappeared in the big musicals in 1933 (see Chapter 5). The lavishness of the musicals was new; the unwavering drabness of the gang world had disappeared.

One estimate of gang films asserted that their "naturalistic detail was in effect a tacit statement that the slum, and therefore society, was responsible for uncontrolled crime." [27] But this evaluation, influenced by the juvenile delinquent environmental orientation of the late thirties, missed the key point. A contemporary analysis was closer to the mark in noting that the gang films were unconcerned with "conditions" breeding crime. "In almost every portrayal of criminals," wrote Edgar Dale, "they appear ready-made . . . full grown. Only rarely was there any indication that criminal patterns of behavior develop as a product of a long process of interaction between the individual and the successive social situations in which he lives." [28]

The causes of crime were not elucidated in the early thirties because there seemed little point to it. Crime was a life style, a way of existing in the world. It was a living. In 1930, its causes were no more at issue than the causes for doctors and musicians. The makers of *The Public Enemy* attempted to speak of causes until they realized they had nothing to say; the vitality of outlaws was self-justifying.

Gangsters would be portrayed in films after 1932, of course, but they could no longer inhabit a world of their own. They became pseudobusinessmen, passing into society and building fronts or they were simply on the run from a renascent law.[29] The early thirties' world of enclosed criminality had vanished. The gangster, Robert Warshow had observed, was "the man of the city . . . not the real city, but that dangerous and sad city of the imagination which is so much more important, which is the modern world." [30] That city was taken from the gangsters for the rest of the decade; later films concerned with crime gave it to juvenile delinquents who became delinquent because of an "environment," which, when altered by a wise and compassionate society, would result in the good life. Unlike the mobsters, the delinquents could be socialized—a priest or social worker would do the trick.

But Rico's Club Palermo, which had only been a mirage of Carnegie's pleasure dome, was shut down. And the society that demanded its closing never escaped the dream of individual and separate success it had asked gangsters to act out.

2

The Shyster and the City

Between 1930 and 1933, a great many films appeared that concerned themselves with corrupt and racy people who lived and worked in the city. These "shyster" films—centering around the activities of lawyers, politicians, and newspapermen—were similar to the gang films in that they also assigned a feckless role to the law. Unlike the gang films, their protagonists were given no tragic dimensions. "Shyster" films were most immediately concerned with corruption, in all its dimensions: the individual chiseling of the dishonest lawyer, and the larger moral weakness of the city in which he operated. Yet their footing was never too sure. Movies like *The Mouthpiece, Lawyer Man, The Front Page*, and *The Dark Horse* seemed to be as drawn to slick double-dealing as they were ostensibly repelled by it. Their makers delighted in the rogues they were attempting to condemn. And this ambivalence was tied not only to the dismal position occupied by the law in 1931 and 1932 but to the fact that in depicting shysters during the nadir of the Depression, they were administering relief, rather than addressing a central problem. In 1932, corruption must have seemed like an old and trusted friend.

Americans have always been fascinated by corruption, simultaneously attracted and outraged, especially when major and disrupting changes are taking place in the society at large. It seems self-evident to note that the country's chief dilemma in 1932 was not the hand in the till, but rather the emptiness of the till. The process by which Hollywood constructed the shyster cycle and created a caricature vision of the city goes well beyond that simple evasion. For the rest of the decade, movies would react to the portrait of the city they had created in the early thirties and to those men with the slicked-down hair and little mustaches who seemed to have so much to do with what was wrong in America. Understand the shysters and their city and one has the key to much of Hollywood's relation to the Depression.

THE SHYSTER'S GOTHAM

"New York is not popular in the United States at large," observed *The Nation* in 1929. "Other places are a little jealous and a little afraid of it. But it is the city to which, if possible, all Americans come some time before they die." [1] The simple duality, of attraction and revulsion, lay at the heart of the New York myth and its effect upon the rest of the country. New York's qualities, wrote sociologist Anselm Strauss, "seem to sum up all the negative balances in the rural animus against the cities. . . ." And yet, as *The Nation* noted, it was the "Mecca and the model of the continent." [2] In the late twenties and early thirties, writers in the popular magazines debated whether New York was "American." Ford Maddox Ford's strange 1927 opus about the city was entitled *New York Is Not America:* "The American who settles in New York becomes at once an ex-American." [3] Variations on the theme were "What Is America?" and "Is New York American?" All articles dealing with these questions placed the nation's feelings toward New York under the heading of love-hate.

Contrasting images of the city bred the mixed feelings: the city as dynamo, the city as moral pollutant. It was the paradigm case of American initiative ("There is no place in the country where one finds more . . . restless energy . . . and devotion to material suc-

cess") and also a foreign land the boroughs of which teemed with
"new immigrant stock." (As a Des Moines newsman put it in Phillip Stong's pro-rural novel of 1932, *State Fair:* "It's God's greatest
gift to mankind except for the dirt, Tammany, dagoes and sub-
ways.") Its very presence tantalized the "ambitious and the eager,
the want-to-be-wealthy and the would-be smart," but it likewise
catered to the "morally and intellectually fatuous of the whole
country." Its "foreignness" crippled Alfred E. Smith's efforts to
become President, wrote Elmer Davis one year after the 1928 elec-
tion; the books and magazines New York produced, *The New
Republic* stated, were considered "demoralizing to the morals of
youth." Ultimately, Earl Sparling concluded in *Scribner's,* New
York was the "mirror in which America . . . suddenly sees itself
for what she is." [4]

So New York was seen as a place of extremes. The citadel of
competitiveness, but vaguely foreign and a trap to the unknowing.
And if Americans longed for and loathed this dreamy and abrasive
place, such contradictory impulses were only fostered and reinforced by the city conjured by Hollywood. That city was exclusively
Gotham—a world inhabited strictly by shysters. It was a caricature
that bred more caricature.

This city could be identified as follows: opening shot of lower
Manhattan's skyline (boats steaming past in the harbor) or Broadway, electric in the night; to shots of society people (long gowns,
tails, silk hats) promenading after the theatre. They stepped into
limousines or honking taxicabs manned by men in caps and sped
off to a nightclub or penthouse. The nightclub was smoky and
peopled by women with blond hair who did fast dancing and sat
on the laps of men with mustaches. They laughed a lot. The penthouse overlooked a section of skyline (squares of lighted windows
painted on the backdrop) and had a balcony on which stood corrupt lawyers with Anglo-Saxon names, politicians with Irish names,
and women with shiny shoulders and low-cut evening gowns.

Deals were made. Standing on the sidewalk below were men
with pads, pencils, and snap-brim hats who told other men holding
cameras to "Get ready, here he comes." These people were news-

papermen, who "phoned in" to "the chief" (a man they hated but loved) and made a great many wisecracks. They were portrayed best by actors like Walter Catlett and Roscoe Karnes. When they "smelled a rat" they were usually correct. They were the picaresque figures of Hollywood's city and would be worth talking about.

A CITY OF NEWSPAPERMEN

The newspaper office was a great place in Depression films. Alcoholic star reporters pestered their grouchy editors, while saucy girl reporters leaned on desks and begged for assignments. Newspapermen, by definition, were after scandal; their corruption was less a matter of graft (phony expense accounts maybe) than a corruption of communication. They lied. The titles of newspaper films—*Scandal For Sale*, *Five-Star Final*, *Scandal Sheet*, *The Front Page*—indicate their wonderfully hysterical tone and subject matter.

Two major character types were evolved in the newspaper film: the slick scandal-crazed editor or publisher and the cynical, puckish ace reporter or gossip columnist. The most grotesque example of the first type was portrayed in *Scandal Sheet* (1931). Its crass editor, George Bancroft, is so profoundly committed to scandal that, after murdering his adulterous wife, he marches back to the city room and dictates the story before giving himself up to the police! (The story was based roughly on the life of Charles Chapin, editor of the New York *Evening Post*.) [5] Less bizarre was Adolphe Menjou's masterful portrait of suave Walter Burns in Lewis Milestone's remarkable film of Ben Hecht's and Charles MacArthur's play, *The Front Page*. Walter Burns was the ultimate editor—breathing sophistication, unsurprised by the scandal he demanded around the clock.

The picaresque reporters—as in *The Front Page* and Frank Capra's 1931 *Platinum Blonde* (both pictures released by Columbia)—skirted about all levels of society. They played the city like virtuosi, unfazed by any social strata, but cynical of all. Their stories were based on all the shyster assumptions about how the world worked: who was on the take, who was sneaking around with whose wife. In *The Front Page*, a half-dozen reporters sit around a press room and watch a half-crazy little anarchist named Earl Williams (George E. Stone) surrender limply to spectacularly inept police, under the command of a corrupt and imbecilic sheriff. On six separate phones, they phone in six separate versions of the event they are witnessing: "After a fierce struggle," "Snarling at his captors." It is a great moment in American film.

Public fascination with Walter Winchell, who was, via syndicated column and radio program, an imposing cultural phenomenon and social influence of the time, led to a cycle of gossip column films in 1932 and 1933: *Is My Face Red, Blessed Event,* and *Okay, America.* And the gossip column appeared throughout the other shyster films, commenting on the action like a leering chorus. But the gossip column was part of the corruption; it was not outside it. The column lived on sensation and was part of the general moral softening that caused politicians and lawyers to turn crooked. In the late thirties, *The New Yorker* profiled Winchell and expressed the premises that really went behind all the shyster films:

> The acceptance and encouragement of gossip and all that gossip stands for is one of the innumerable results of the disappearance of a . . . sure, unquestioning intolerance toward the mean, the petty, the unfair, the cheap. . . . We seem to have adopted a sort of anything goes philosophy.[6]

The moralism was Hollywood's; the aristocratic disdain was not —movie shysters were far too lovable. And the newspaper films helped define Hollywood's city because the articulation of corruption as a central problem in 1932 required the building of an artificial city to support it.

But even clichéd images of the city can be used to make genuine points about the quality of urban life, though few films bothered to try. For instance, the subway and its straphangers have been part of the pat New York City image. When King Kong starts dismembering New York, the elevated line is the first to go. But Lewis Mumford could ride the subway, feel and see the "stale air, the press of warm bodies, the distorted postures, the complete inanity of the ride" and make a social point:

. . . as a daily occurrence New York's rush hour is incredible. . . .
What callous patches must form on the personality before these criminal rushes can be accepted as part of the inevitable routine of living!
One can only account for the subway by remembering that pathology
often masquerades as a mode of life . . . so in our great cities, this daily
degradation may have the outward appearance of purposive activity. . . .
All this skyscraper-building and tunnel digging . . . this human waste
and futility is justified by the canons of finance—and the metropolis
knows no other standard.[7]

Except for King Vidor, whose 1928 masterpiece, *The Crowd,*
had a lot to do with what Mumford was talking about, no one in
Hollywood operated to allow this real city to appear on screen.
Only Vidor (see Chapter 6) seemed to share Mumford's vision of
the inexorable beating down of the individual into a cipher whose
life was defined by forces over which he had no control. Vidor's
hero was trapped in mass work (a huge office—endless desks manned
by faceless clerks) and mass fun (Coney Island, company picnics).
The effect on screen was devastating.

Images of the city that were accessible to all could have been
used by filmmakers to illuminate some real social difficulties; Vidor
proved it. But images of urban "glamor" and petty crime—easy
marks for melodramatic treatment—predominated. Earl Sparling
had struck a vein of such imagery when he said of New York: "I
despise its graft, its crime, its dirt, its opportunistic cheapness, its
parvenu swank. . . ."[8] An army of character actors and extras
waited in the wings, wearing evening clothes or striped suits and
derbies, their little mustaches daubed on. If something was wrong
with the cities and America, they were apparently behind it. As
the economic order collapsed, forces in the culture alerted citizens
to the hand in the cash drawer.

SHYSTER LAWYERS AND SHYSTER POLITICIANS

Lawyer Man (Warner, 1932. Director, William Dieterle)
The Mouthpiece (Warner, 1932. Directors, James Flood & Elliot
Nugent)

State's Attorney (RKO Radio. Director, George Archambaul)
The Dark Horse (Warner, 1932. Director, Alfred E. Green)
The Phantom President (Paramount, 1932. Director, Norman
   Taurog)
Washington Masquerade (MGM, 1932. Director, Charles Brabin)
   Two longish quotations seem instructive:

BLOWS THE LID OFF!

Never before in our national history has the American public been
so critical of its political representatives as it is today. [*Washington
Merry-Go-Round*] is a direct reflection of the new standard of Americanism which has come into being during the recent years of depression
and hardship. The point . . . is that the people are the losers because
of our system which makes many of our representatives self-seekers,
rather than servers of their country.[9]

                                                    —MGM press book, 1932

In the depth of the American winter, on a day when a stabbing icy
wind pierced the thickest overcoat, I saw the unemployed living on
wastelands, in shacks put together from old boxes (wood and tin), bits
of old motor cars, bits of corrugated iron, bits of cloth. I saw them
lining up nearly three sides of a block waiting in a queue for soup. I
saw them scrounging over refuse heaps like flies crawling over a dung
hill. Even in India I had not seen destitution more horrible or humili-
ating.[10]

                                                    —English observer, 1933

The British observer gazing upon the miserable St. Louis shanty
town in 1933 and the MGM press agent assessing the fallen republic, despite their vastly differing tones, were aware of the same
dismal truths. Hollywood saw as its task the conversion of the
nation's broken hopes and seemingly insoluble dilemmas into a
comprehensible cause and effect. The end result was barely recog-
nizable as the United States. It was true that Americans were
critical of their political representatives—the touch of shyster
alchemy was to transmute their despair into a "new standard of
Americanism" which blamed politicians for going through the
public pockets. Never had the government gotten off easier. The

nation's critique, in truth, involved no consideration of wrong-doing, but rather a muteness in the face of disaster. People shrank from the enormity of it all. "America's ills," writes labor historian Irving Bernstein, "were melancholia and hypochondria, not revolution. . . . Louis Adamic and Benjamin Stolberg agreed that the American proletariat was physically and spiritually exhausted." Arthur Schlesinger, Jr., summed up the American mood in 1932 as "less one of revolt than of apathy. People were sullen rather than bitter." [11] More citizens became jobless, hopeless, and empty of will, so empty that their most popular art form could not bear to look. Yet the shyster cycle evolved out of this growing stillness; its obsession with corruption was rooted in uncertainty. "The Depression," writes Bernstein, "was hard to see with the naked eye . . . the jobless stayed off the streets." [12] Into this strange quiet came crooked lawyers and crooked politicians, in a desperate attempt to show what was really wrong.

Makers of films about shyster lawyers operated on the assumption that things in the society *were* seriously wrong and that the former verities were fast disappearing; yet the dynamics of plot invariably defined the dislocations as rooted in graft. The protagonists of *State's Attorney* (John Barrymore, modeled after William Fallon, the flashiest lawyer of the 1920s), *The Mouthpiece* (Warren William, likewise modeled on Fallon) and *Lawyer Man* (William Powell) all waltz through shyster city with aplomb. Women love them; the gossip columns report their doings with regularity. But all three renounce their shyster practices and walk away from the defense of mobsters and political bosses. (Caricatures defended other caricatures; none of the movie lawyers did much corporate work.) Warren William, after reels of very funny legal razzle-dazzle on behalf of hoodlums and embezzlers, declares, "They thought they owned me. I'm going back to civil practice. I'm tired of crooked streets and crooked people." Barrymore, with mob and gambling connections, lurches through a drunken marriage to a debutante, and ends by going "back where I belong," defending clients who "start in the gutter." Powell returns "back to my people," to protect them from "political bosses."

Lawyer Man is the shyster film most rooted in the social world

Hollywood constructed to nurture and protect its guiding thesis about the ills of the nation. Starting with a humble practice among "his people" on the Lower East Side, Powell is tempted into partnership with a sharp and wealthy Park Avenue lawyer. Refusing to "play along" with a political boss, he is framed by an intricate trap involving the boss, a corrupt judge, and a girl. The experience embitters him and turns him crooked. He blames the city for his new morality: "Every guy for himself . . . the town's full of them. . . . Boost the guy who's riding high. . . . They made a shyster out of me. . . . I'll show them." But after having tasted the life of a corrupt swell by defending the moral dregs of the city (and even forbidding his secretary to open his windows, for fear of allowing in fresh air), he renounces it all to return to the Lower East Side. He vows to protect those who are having "their rights trampled on" by the political bosses.

Such a plot resolution was clear-cut and reinforcing. Since political rights only were being abused, some forthright work on behalf of the democratic process would set the social order straight again. Going back "to the gutter" and fighting the bosses invoked the old absolutes. Acting out control over "politics" for audiences increasingly struck by their utter lack of control over the forces that determined food, clothing, and shelter was perhaps Hollywood's most desperate fantasy of the early thirties. Given headline "realism" by such scandals as the Jimmy Walker hearings, and historicity by progressive attacks upon political machines, the plot resolutions of the lawyer films were as distant from social facts as Shirley Temple dancing down the stairs with Bojangles Bill Robinson.

(A further note on films about lawyers. They are clearly marked "Depression" not only by the gross caricature of social dislocation, but by the laughing-stock image they conveyed of the law. Powell, Barrymore, and William, by operating through the loopholes of the law, used legal codes as the straight man for an ongoing joke. Press copy for *The Mouthpiece* noted that dishonest lawyers could "practice without disbarment because they operate within the law, despite their illegal connections." [13] "Within the law" became meaningless in the light of their seamy machinations; the law again came off as a vacuum.)

In the films centering on shyster politicos another premise was added, one that would linger throughout the thirties. Not only was politics placed on the familiar and controllable grounds of corruption, but the populace (despite the rhetoric of *Washington Merry-Go-Round*'s press copy) was portrayed as gullible to every political prank—an easy tool for shysters. As the thirties film evolved and Warner Brothers began to dramatize social ills (see Chapter 8), the erratic and untrustworthy nature of the average citizen became strongly implicit in films like *Black Fury* (1935), *Black Legion* (1937), *Fury* (1936), and *They Won't Forget* (1937). This public volatility, in the mid-thirties, spoke to the need for a strong, righteous and alert national government, and federal benevolence was added to Hollywood convention. In movies about dishonest politicians, an ignorant public was easily swayed by guile.

In 1931's Pulitzer Prize winning musical, *Of Thee I Sing*, a presidential candidate comments on Lincoln's admonition against fooling the people: "It's different nowadays. People are bigger suckers." [14] Hollywood demonstrated similar sentiments. In *The Dark Horse*, an extremely funny and bitter film about electoral politics, the protagonist is a political wheeler-dealer (again Warren William, one of the early thirties' most endearing and valuable comic actors) who is recruited out of jail to manage a gubernatorial campaign. His candidate (Guy Kibee) is an imbecile dark horse nominee. "He's the dumbest human being I ever saw," says William of the nominee. "We're going to convince the voters that they're getting one of them. That's what voters want in these days of corruption and depression." As always, "corruption" and "depression" were harnessed together. The candidate, trained to answer "Yes, and then again, No" to every question, wins in a landslide.

Released during the presidential contest of 1932, *The Dark Horse* reduced electoral politics to a battle of connivers. (So did *The Phantom President*, released around the same time. Revolving around a case of mistaken identity—between presidential candidate and medicine show spieler—it concluded that the two were, in fact,

interchangeable.) The cynicism, such as it was, worked two ways. If
politics were laughable, so was the citizenry which played straight
man; for people to mock their leaders, they had to mock themselves. The bitterness of the period surfaces here far more markedly
than in the other shyster films, yet the release these films provided
could only be limited. The most audacious political spoof of the
decade (and probably of American film), the Marx Brothers'
Duck Soup (see Chapter 3), attacked not the connivings of politics, but the idea of politics. The wild success of the Marxes
in 1931 and 1932 demonstrated how open these subjects were for
attack in those years. But the shyster satires, despite some genuine
bite, were essentially cautious vehicles for mocking political life.
Their focus on corruption narrowed the possibilities for relevance
to the deepest woes of the early thirties; they reacted more to a
political world Hollywood had itself created.

"Serious" films about politics never even approached the limited
relevance of the comedies. A film like *Washington Masquerade*
was totally bogged down in images of corruption and the amoral
city. Washington became exclusively a nest of rapacious lobby-
ists ("inside details of the 'lobbyist' rackets . . . the shadowy
figures of intrigue in the political arena,") [15] a city of *femmes
fatales* and lurid bargains. Its righteous, craggy Senator (Lionel
Barrymore) is elected by his state's "good government" forces
and deceived almost instantly by a mustachioed agent of the
power industry, who bribes him out of a public power crusade.
Karen Morley's sizzling charms complete the scrambling of Barrymore's brains and good intentions.

Before dying of heart failure, Barrymore pins the blame for
his downfall at a Senate hearing. His speech is a fine example of
the gymnastics the shyster films performed to justify their existence. After the lobbyist has rationalized the private power grab
by explaining that "the business of the country had to be taken
out of the hands of Congress," Barrymore arises and, voice quavering, brings the film to a patriotic conclusion with this curious
rhetoric: "Take the people's business out of Congress, huh! There's
a man in the White House whose heart is broken because we're
traitors." Hoover stricken by shysterism; the graying man in the

White House sold out by corrupt congressmen. Even granting the staunch Republicanism of MGM's studio head, Louis B. Mayer,[16] it was a notably perverse interpretation of the world outside. Let decent men legislate and "these days of corruption and depression" would vanish like a mirage. The only economics Hollywood could associate with political life was graft, money changing hands, in 1932.

Shysterism, then, was the film industry's attempt to make dislocation visible and give it a clearly labelled cause—one that could be changed by simple righteousness. The shyster city remained "the city" until the end of the decade, when juvenile delinquent films made it into an "environment." And the caricatures of evil first-movers would do much to cripple Warner Brothers' series of "topical" films in the mid-thirties. Hollywood could never quite escape the feeling that there had to be a tangible villain somewhere.

3

Some Anarcho-Nihilist Laff Riots

Perhaps it was his experience as a member of Warren Harding's Cabinet that made Will Hays think he was an authority on comedy. For whatever reason, he was able to prophecy, in his 1934 *Annual Report* to the MPPDA, that "historians of the future will note the . . . fact that the movies literally laughed the big bad wolf of the depression out of the public mind." [1] It was a reassuring thought. After a long day on the soupline or after being thrown off his farm, the citizen could gather his family and amble down to the Strand, to relax in the plush and chuckle away disaster. But there was a stream of film comedy in the early thirties that had little to do with chasing away bad wolves: an anarchic stream in which meaning and meaninglessness fused, in which the pun routed rational dialogue. Spiritual forerunners of those who would create the theatre of the absurd in the 1950s, The Marx Brothers and W. C. Fields exhibited little of the good-natured horseplay implied by Will Hays. Much of Hollywood's highest art had been comic: it should not be so surprising that in the early thirties the movies most related to the bitterness and despair in America be comedies.

THE MARX BROTHERS

They were Chico, Groucho, Harpo, and Zeppo. The Depression did not create their comedy; that craft had been mastered by years on the road, playing vaudeville stages and Broadway. But the Depression endorsed it and made it a national pastime.

Chico, his stagy Italian accent a heritage from the great days of dialect comedy, mangled English usage, arranged malapropisms, and made conversation completely impossible. Harpo came on as an impulsive lunatic—grabbing chambermaids and dancing with them suddenly and frantically, the music in his head. From his pockets appeared scissors, blowtorches, table service, cups of coffee, and the horn with which he communicated. Zeppo, the straight man where none was needed, mainly stood around and was dropped after *Duck Soup*. And Groucho, the very raise of whose eyebrows was a statement, was a man who had erased the boundaries between logic and illogic, for whom disorder was an assumption rather than a problem. He was in some ways the traditional American "wiseacre," the town prankster.

The prank in Marx films became a system unto itself and was all-inclusive. Language became a prank. Every dialogue between Chico and Groucho became conversational feedback and fuzz. In *The Cocoanuts*, Groucho tries to explain the location of a viaduct. "Why a duck," asks Chico again and again. Groucho finally admits he doesn't know why a duck. In *Animal Crackers*, the two discuss the search for a stolen painting:

G: Suppose nobody in the house took the painting?
C: Go to the house next door.
G: Suppose there isn't any house next door?
C: Then we gotta build one.

While the games played with language stemmed from old burlesque traditions of the malapropism, dialect confusion, and the verbal pratfall, the brothers made word play an art. Misunderstanding and understanding were identical.

From 1929 to 1933, the Marxes made five films for Paramount—
The Cocoanuts (1929), *Animal Crackers* (1930), *Monkey Business*
(1931), *Horsefeathers* (1932), and *Duck Soup* (1933)—and gave
new life to the words "chaos" and "shambles." They had reached
great heights on Broadway in the revues, *The Cocoanuts* and
Animal Crackers, when their agent, William Morris, convinced
Paramount's Jesse Lasky that the brothers were naturals for the
screen. In those early days of talkies, many of Chico's dialect
mumblings and Groucho's rapid-fire snappers were unintelligible
on the sound track. After they were shown the final cut of *The
Cocoanuts*, the Marxes were so appalled that they attempted to
buy the negative back. Paramount resisted, and the film made a
profit of close to two million dollars.[2]

Animal Crackers was Paramount's biggest moneymaker in 1930,
and people began to perceive that the Marxes represented a kind
of gloriously American liberation from convention. The French
critic and playwright, Antonin Artaud, pronounced *Animal
Crackers* an "extraordinary thing" and saw in it

the liberation through the medium of the screen of a particular magic
which the ordinary relation of words and images does not customarily
reveal, and if there is a definite characteristic, a distinct poetic state of
mind that can be called *surrealism*, *Animal Crackers* participated in that
state altogether.[3]

Yet Artaud doubted if Americans would see the metaphysical
implications of the Marxes' horseplay. Being literal-minded people, the chances were they would "take these films in a merely
humorous sense." Yet it was clear that the brothers were produc-
ing a "hymn to anarchy and whole-hearted revolt."[4] The terms
of the revolt were not clear, and the raise of Groucho's giant eyebrows not the exact equivalent to the unfurling of a red flag, but
the wild reception of the Marxes' chaos between 1930 and 1933
seems no accident.

Artaud perhaps had good reason to be skeptical of American
movie audiences. The review of *Animal Crackers* in the *Motion
Picture Herald* was not encouraging: "It is all nonsense, of course,

but nobody cares. It is all silly but everybody laughs." [5] It was all silly. Yet no matter how dim the surface reaction, the films were produced and wildly received in a specific context, for from 1930 to 1934, a number of "silly" films, with next to no plot, appeared in our movie theatres as the economy sank out of sight.

Will Hays had surely not meant that Americans were escaping into pure Dada. Yet the success of disjunctive, chaotic efforts that mocked intelligibility seems to reveal a nation not so much searching for silliness as one capable of sensing the absurdity of the verities and relations that had been treasured before. Obviously, this might be an overgeneralization, and one does not suggest a nation of fledgling Ionescos, but the fact remains that absurdity has never had it so good in American film since that time.

Million Dollar Legs (Paramount, 1932. Director, Edward Cline)

Million Dollar Legs is a plotless pastiche of ancient slapstick and sight gags that utilized nationhood and the Olympic Games for manic purposes. The *Motion Picture Herald* accurately observed that Paramount had "gone back into the dark ages of motion pictures" [6] in resurrecting the aesthetics of the Keystone comedies. The ludicrous national setting was Klopstockia, a land subsisting on the export of goats and nuts. Its president, W. C. Fields, holds office via an electoral process that requires him to win at Indian wrestling each morning. An uneasy head of state, he sits at cabinet meetings with a gun and brass knuckles, as totally incomprehensible intrigues are plotted against him. The film is a string of *non sequiturs*. Jack Oakie portrays a travelling brush salesman considered subversive by Fields' opponents. He croons the Klopstockian love song, "Wolf-boogle-gik" and learns that all Klopstockian men are named George and all women, Angela. The nation goes to the Olympics. Fields appears in gym togs, constantly spied upon by the great cross-eyed silent comedian, Ben Turpin. Government is reduced to a kind of vaudeville. In *Million Dollar Legs*, the sight humor and verbal gags seem to run independently of each other, creating an effect both unsettling and very funny. The film manages to reduce everything it considers (like spying and statehood) to a kind of accident.

Million Dollar Legs was a box office success in the late summer of 1932.⁷ Its success, together with the huge success of the early Marx pictures, indicates that its form was attractive. It was not merely the personality of the Marxes which brought people to their films, but rather, the kind of action the brothers loosed.

Groucho's position changed during the course of the Depression. In the early films, he had been an outsider. In *The Cocoanuts*, he ran a fading Florida hotel and auctioned off swampy real estate; *Animal Crackers* presented him as Jeffrey Spaulding, the fortune-hunting and cowardly African explorer (rhymed with "schnorrer"); in *Monkey Business*, he was merely a stowaway on a boat.

Yet in 1932 and 1933, of all times, Groucho achieved a dizzying rise in position, if not stature. In 1932, Paramount released *Horsefeathers* and placed him, as Quincy Adams Wagstaff, at the head of Huxley College. At his inaugural, Groucho sat on stage shaving. So much for education; he and his brothers stage some early campus disruptions. The ascension of Groucho to this position of authority was only a dry run for *Duck Soup*, when as prime minister he would attempt to run the land of Freedonia into the ground. More confined in *Horsefeathers*, he could only dismember a university. But in 1933, Groucho, as Rufus T. Firefly, assumed effective non-leadership of Freedonia. Not since Woodrow Wilson had the step from university leadership to national power been made with such consummate ease.

Duck Soup was the most fully orchestrated attack upon the sanctity of the state ever to reach the American screen. But the public that had flocked to *Animal Crackers* and would fill theatres for *A Night At The Opera* in 1935, just would not support *Duck Soup*, the Marx Brothers' most audacious film.

It was not just the general populace. American critics also failed to grasp what the application of the Marxes to a political situation ultimately implied. The New York *Herald-Tribune's* Richard Watts, Jr., at this time a fairly outspoken leftist critic of film, claimed that "American experts at satirical farce are not at their best when mocking the frailties of dictatorship" and concluded that the brothers were not concerned with "providing a significant social comment." [8] *The New York Times* found *Duck Soup* "almost impossible to follow." [9] But the most symptomatic critique came from William Troy, writing in *The Nation:*

The present story might have been shaped into a hilarious burlesque of dictatorship; but this would have amounted to humor with a point, and the essence of Marxian humor is its pointlessness. . . . It consists of a disassociation of the faculties rather than a concentrated direction of them toward a particular object in the body social or politic.[10]

The middle thirties were not the time for abstract mockings of statehood. What *The Nation* wanted was an attack upon dictatorship, a satiric crusade against political evil. But *Duck Soup* was an attack against political anything; it came out of the deepest cynicism about all government. What is perfectly clear after ten minutes of the film is that the whole idea of statehood and national loyalty is preposterous. The very idea of political action becomes a bad joke. (While *The Nation* felt *Duck Soup* had missed its chance to burlesque dictatorship, Benito Mussolini felt it had done quite well. The film was banned in Italy.) [11]

In *Duck Soup*, Prime Minister Firefly ("A fearless, progressive leader") has been handpicked by the dowager Mrs. Teasedale (Margaret Dumont—the butt of a thousand gags) to run Freedonia. He does not hesitate to demean both his office and his duties immediately. He slides down a fire pole into his inaugural ceremony, where he does pointless card tricks and asks the ambassador from neighboring Sylvania for a personal loan of twelve dollars. Presiding over the Chamber of Deputies, Rufus plays jacks. He reluctantly stops in order to begin the meeting, during which he refuses to consider either old or new business, declares himself unable to read a treasury report and bullies a minister into quitting. He convinces Chico to give up his peanut stand for a "soft government job." When Chico insults him, he is made Secretary of War. Riddles are substituted for civil service exams. The apparatus of government is gleefully dismantled.

The most important game is the war game, and the great part of this short film is taken up with the degenerating relationship between Freedonia and Sylvania, a deterioration accelerated by Firefly's outrageous defense of personal honor. When Mrs. Teasedale announces that the Sylvanian ambassador is coming to apologize for an earlier "insult," Rufus works himself into a rage, arriving at the conclusion that he "is coming to make a sap out of me." Firefly stakes the prestige of Freedonia upon the totally fabricated assumption that the ambassador is coming *not* to shake hands with him. When the ambassador arrives, Rufus cries, "So you refuse to shake hands with me," and slaps his face. And the war came.

The handshake issue was a beautiful parody of the kind of protocol lapses, flag incidents, and so on, that have been maneuvered into pretexts for carnage. By such trifles do nations define their honor. Freedonia gaily plunges into war as the massed populace sings "We're Going To War," led by the Marxes. They put the patriotic anthem through a series of changes, nasally twanging "Comin' Round the Mountain," phasing into minstrel style and clapping their hands and waving them to "All God's Chillun Got Guns." The citizens follow their leader's every move. When Rufus stands on his hands, they stand on theirs. Patriotism becomes a game of Simon Says.

Having made loyalty a grotesque pose, the Marxes dispose of war in a series of sequences which are nothing so much as a vaudeville *All Quiet On The Western Front*. The cutting edge was very sharp, the brothers' attitude being expressed when Harpo is sent across "enemy lines" (Harpo and Chico keep switching sides) in the heat of battle. As he heads out, Rufus declares, "While you're out there risking life and limb . . . we'll be in here thinking what a sucker you are." Having made the war pointless politically, he makes it pointless personally. One is fighting neither for a cause nor for personal glory. One is fighting because one is fighting.

And one fights because that's what countries are supposed to do. The war sequences are "historical." The Marxes emerge in different costumes: as revolutionaries, redcoats, rebels, union men, frontier coonskinners, Allied Expeditionary Forces. Sides are irrelevant: the uniforms are obviously costumes, get-ups, rather than symbols of side or cause. The tragicomedy of it all is summed up by Rufus when he is informed he is firing on his own men: "Here's five dollars, keep it under you hat. Never mind, I'll keep it under my hat." And when Freedonia has "won" the war, Mrs. Tease-dale bursts into "Hail, Hail Freedonia" and the brothers bombard her with fruit. It is a perfect finale: nationhood supreme in victory beaten down by a hail of oranges.

When *Duck Soup* was distributed to local theatres early in 1934, it was generally met with hostility. The manager of a Nebraska movie house complained "Even a small town knows when there is a flop. This was sure it." Joe Hewitt, who ran the Lincoln Theatre in Robinson, Illinois, saw it as "a lot of gags and chatter that did not appeal to the masses. Draw was much less than previous Marx release." "Silly, disgusting," was one reaction from Anadarko, Oklahoma, and a theatre manager in Ellinwood, Iowa, was "afraid these boys are washed up." [12] At least three managers were unhappy over Harpo's failure to play the harp and the absence of Chico's piano routines.

Yet surely *Duck Soup* did not fare poorly just because it lacked musical interludes. Were people getting tired of the Marxes? The great box office success of their next two films, *A Night At The Opera* (MGM, 1935) and *A Day At The Races* (MGM, 1937) seems to rule that out. Was it that the moviegoing public was loathe to see political institutions mocked? *Million Dollar Legs*, *The Dark Horse* and *The Phantom President*, as well as shyster politico films, demonstrated that the government was a fit target in 1931 and 1932.

The seemingly anomalous failure of what is perhaps the Marx Brothers' finest film is most likely explained by its timing. After a year of Roosevelt's energy and activism, government, no matter what else it might be, was no absurdity. The New Deal would breed its own myths in film, but in 1934 it seems to have utterly cut the ground from under Groucho as prime minister. Furthermore, as the Watts and Troy critiques make clear, the social consciousness that was permeating Eastern intellectual life could not abide the absolute destructiveness of the Marxes.

A new kind of comedy became popular in 1934, with the unexpected and gigantic success of Frank Capra's *It Happened One Night*. Labelled "screwball" comedy, it stressed a breezy nuttiness that worked to pull things (marriages, social classes) together, rather than break them apart. It dominated film comedy for the rest of the decade. At another time, maybe the Grouchos could assume power, but for the time being they were relegated to more limited spheres. The public still loved the Marxes, so long as they knew their place. They did. In *A Night At The Opera*, Groucho plays a jobless opera impresario; in *A Day At The Races*, a seedy horse doctor; in *Room Service*, a penniless Broadway producer.

W. C. FIELDS AND "THE FATAL GLASS OF BEER"

No look at the anarcho-nihilist films of the early thirties can ignore the W. C. Fields short, *The Fatal Glass Of Beer*. A comic masterpiece, it was filled with cynicism about two treasured American institutions: the family and the frontier. The family is a sham; the frontier is a place nitwits get stuck in.

Fields was such a genius that he could bring it all off in twenty minutes. A study of absurdist drama called this runaway from a Philadelphia home a "brilliant Surrealist comedian," and James Agee saw Fields as "the one great comedian of the talkie era." [13] His ability to sense the crippling pettiness of daily life was nothing less than magical and his art was never purer than in the four shorts he made for Mack Sennett in 1933. In *The Pharmacist*, *The Dentist* and *The Barbershop*, Fields painted the funniest and saddest portraits of small town life imaginable. His druggist wrapped stamps in paper bags and freely distributed huge vases; his barber, the local sadist, was a badgered man who strapped patrons into their chairs before dropping blazing towels on their faces. His bogus dignity was unshakable; his view of the hounded head of the family shattering.

In *The Fatal Glass Of Beer*, Fields the frontiersman is forced to cope with a series of strange disorders. His only son Chester has run off to the city, had some beer and then embezzled bonds. We learn this in the form of a ballad sung by Fields to a weeping Canadian mountie. Fields accompanies himself on a zither, wearing gloves. Chester suddenly comes home and his father runs around the cabin in joy, his foot caught in a bucket. The pathos attendant upon Chester's return is quick-frozen into a ghastly bedtime ritual. The members of the family address each other as if speaking from separate mountaintops. The good-night ceremony involves:

Good night, Pa.
Good night, Chester.
Good night, Ma.
Good night, Chester.
Sleep well, Pa.
I will. You too, Chester.
Sleep well, Ma.
Thank you. You sleep well, Chester.
Don't forget to keep your window open, Chester.
I won't. You remember too, Pa.
I will, Chester. Good night.
Good night, Pa.
Good night.

The constant use of their names, as if to remind themselves who the others are, is a macabre and hysterically funny parody of the family relation. (Fields' childhood was not a happy one and all his films treated family life as a cruel sham.)[14] The *coup de grace* to family ties comes about when Chester admits to having stolen the bonds. His parents thoughtfully forgive him. When he adds that he "threw away all that tainted money," Ma and Pa beat him senseless and toss him into the freezing night. The myth of the home as the last refuge for the beleaguered is thus ruined. If in time of stress one could not lean back upon home and family, what did one have. An obvious answer being inner steadfastness and determination, Fields succeeded in making a travesty of both.

Fields the pioneer is faced with a totally hostile environment. Coping with it is impossible. Snow comes in through the windows of his cabin, cascades from his pockets and falls from his hat into his soup. It is inescapable. Most importantly, the snow flies directly into his face whenever he observes that "It ain't a fit night out for

man or beast." Fields stands stock still when he says this, in a
kind of madman pioneer tableau. Determined, stoic and wooden,
the frontiersman peers straight ahead and appears oblivious to the
hale of snowflakes that lands on his head. This occurs perhaps a
half-dozen times in the movie, and it grows funnier as it
grows more inevitable. Fields obliterates the legend of the pioneer
and the qualities that composed the legend. What could be seen
as steadfastness in the face of hardship becomes obtuseness in the
face of the unavoidable. The tough, silent pioneer is transformed
into a sucker, a dunce. Fields' frontiersman does not cleverly adapt
to his environment: he botches his elk call, maintains a dachshund
on his dog team and still can get nothing better than ice cubes
from the town pump. When he gets hungry out on the trail, he
eats his lead dog: "He was mighty good with mustard." Fields the
frontiersman exists in spite of, rather than because of, his personal
qualities. For, what did personal qualities have to do with a world
in which the snow kept flying in one's face? A comedian like
Charles Chaplin, working contemporaneously with Fields, worked
his comic character against tangible enemies: the rich and the
powerful. Chaplin's world contained great reserves of decency and
innocence which he drew upon with unabashed sentimentality.

Fields saw decency and innocence as at best irrelevant, at worst
positive obstacles. What made his comic intelligence the sharpest
of any American funnyman was his intuition that the "enemy"
was not so easy to find: it appeared to be the whole vague universe.
In the final moment of *Fatal Glass*, Ma and Pa, having deposited
Chester on a snowbank, stare into the distance, as Pa declares,
"Ain't a fit night out. . . ." This time Fields tempts fate and
recoils ever so slightly to avoid the snow. It doesn't come. Man is
a sucker, helpless to do anything about the fact.

The film appeared in the spring of 1933 and got less than an
enthusiastic reception. As Fields admirer William K. Everson
describes it:

"The Fatal Glass Of Beer" was almost universally disliked at the time.
Exhibitors complained that it had no story and no slapstick; audiences
were puzzled, waiting for it to "take off" and go somewhere, which it

never did. All it had was Fields, which in those days was hardly enough. Even confirmed Fields fanciers felt let down by it. Actually, it was another case of a brilliant little film being offered at the wrong time, before the public was attuned to such bizarre and even black comedy.[15]

The most desperate years of our national experience produced our most desperate comedy, one that rang some hilarious and savage changes on a hundred conventions. The freewheeling nihilism of the early Marx and Fields films has not been approached since; the "screwball" comedy of the mid-thirties would stress goodheartedness and social unity. The screen anarchists entertained a bleak and heartsick civilization that expected the worst from everyone. What has been called "zaniness" was really the dark side of American irreverence, a wild response to an unprecedented shattering of confidence.

LITTLE CAESAR. Rico (Edward G. Robinson) explains his success to one-time sidekick Joe Masara (Douglas Fairbanks, Jr.). (Courtesy of United Artists Television.)

LITTLE CAESAR. Rico confronts the law, in the person of Sgt. Flaherty (Thomas Jackson). The sergeant is accompanied by some shadowy underlings. (Courtesy of United Artists Television.)

THE PUBLIC ENEMY. Tommy Powers (James Cagney) prepares to finish off the double-crossing Putty Nose (Murray Kinnell), while sidekick Matt (Edward Woods) warily looks on. (Courtesy of United Artists Television.)

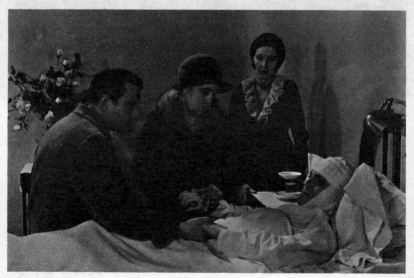

THE PUBLIC ENEMY. A successful gangster was, by definition, a dead gangster. Surrounded by kin (Donald Cook, Beryl Mercer, Louise Brooks), Tommy bows to the inevitable. (Courtesy of United Artists Television.)

THE MOUTHPIECE. This is what a shyster looked like. A Warner Brothers publicity photo of Warren William. (Courtesy of United Artists Television.)

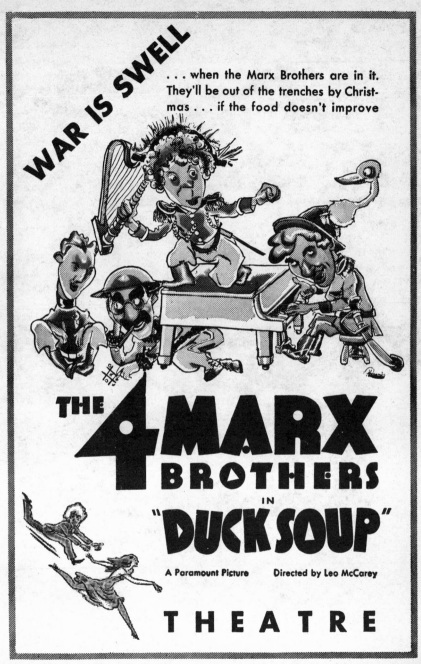

DUCK SOUP. A Paramount poster for DUCK SOUP. (Courtesy of Universal Pictures.)

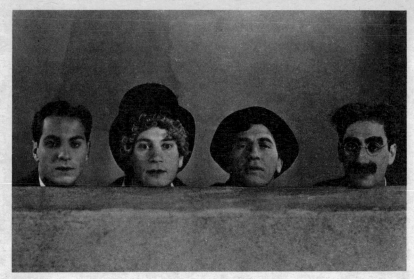

The Marx Brothers: Zeppo, Harpo, Chico and Groucho. (Courtesy of Universal Pictures.)

SHE DONE HIM WRONG. Mae West ensnares yet another suitor. Gilbert Roland offers some diamonds. (Courtesy of Universal Pictures.)

42ND STREET. Stage manager George E. Stone instructs the budding chorines. At extreme right is Ruby Keeler. (Courtesy of United Artists Television.)

GOLD DIGGERS OF 1935. A typical arrangement of dancers by dance director Busby Berkeley. (Courtesy of United Artists Television.)

4

Sex and Personal Relations: Women of the Streets, Women of the World

. . . there is a distinct increase in the number of registered prostitutes during periods of financial depression. . . . I am ready to assert that very often all that is necessary to effectively help the girl who is on the edge of wrong-doing is to lend her money until she finds work.
—Jane Addams, 1912

. . . inability to get work is forcing many young women either directly into prostitution or at least into borderline occupations. . . .
The depression will pass . . . but women forced into vice . . : minds sapped by strain—these won't be cured when prosperity returns.
—New York Committee Of Fourteen, 1932

I must pay tribute to another durable trouper, Mae West, for the powerful lift she gave us out of the depression mire. Neither the sweet

ingenue nor the glamor girl fit the depression years. Mae did. She was
the strong, confident woman, always in command.

—Adolph Zukor,
Paramount Pictures [1]

There *was* a distinct increase in the number of prostitutes, registered and otherwise, who peopled American movies during the
early thirties. A series of films that considered the "fallen woman"
began to reach the theatres in 1931, and such noteworthy protagonists as Tallulah Bankhead, Marlene Dietrich, and Greta
Garbo found themselves in economic straits so severe that their
highly desirable bodies became their only saleable possessions. "By
the third year of the depression," notes one film history, "the
economic independence of women had collapsed almost completely. . . . In the harsh world of supply and demand, they had
nothing to sell but sex." [2]

The "fallen woman" route was the obverse of gangsterism. The
male chose a mobster's life as a means to success; the female opted
for prostitution as the result of continued failure. Both Dietrich
in *Blonde Venus* and Garbo in *Susan Lenox, Her Fall And Rise*
attempt to make do in varying forms of show business, but ultimately must sleep around to keep fed and prosperous.

And the woman's role on film was one of total dependency, the
slave not merely of individual men but of a male society, with no
options for individual action or genuine freedom. In bed or in
the marketplace, the woman could call no tune.

But opposing forces in Hollywood worked toward exploding
not only the grimness of the female role but, up to a point, accepted standards of social relations. Mae West took sex out of the
murky corners of the "fallen women" cycle and made it the target
of a thousand very funny lines. Director Ernst Lubitsch, in films
such as *Design For Living, One Hour With You*, and *Trouble In
Paradise*, played some continental games with the marriage relation. The lines of thought and behavior stretched from prostitute
Dorothy MacKaill's decision, in a film called *Safe In Hell*, to hang
rather than suffer further sexual humiliation, to Mae West's initial
words in her first starring film, *She Done Him Wrong*:

BYSTANDER: You're a fine woman.
MAE: One of the finest women ever walked the streets.

WOMEN OF THE STREETS

Blonde Venus (Paramount, 1932. Director, Josef Von Sterberg)
Faithless (MGM, 1932. Director, Harry Beaumont)
Safe in Hell (Warner, 1931. Director, William Wellman)
Susan Lenox, Her Fall And Rise (MGM, 1931. Director, Robert Z. Leonard)

Dorothy MacKaill in *Safe In Hell* and Tallulah Bankhead in *Faithless* engage in prostitution; the bigger stars, Dietrich and Garbo, are forced to become the mistresses of wealthy men. All of these films involved a woman's willingness to suffer indignities out of an overriding commitment to one man. This is doubtless the stuff of which a million "true confession" tales have been made; what is most intriguing about these films is not the severity of moral punishment such loyalty brings, but the rapid closing out of options for independent action once economic disaster strikes. Ex-millionairess Bankhead, as her broke and ailing husband (Robert Montgomery) lies bedridden, puts on rouge and lipstick and declares, "There isn't anything I won't do." As she exits toward the street, a sympathetic landlady looks on and says, "The things us women do for their men." Dietrich, in *Blonde Venus*, observes her husband dying of radium poisoning and in need of specialists. She gets a cabaret job which features her dressed in a gorilla suit and a grotesque blond wig. Garbo runs away from home and into the arms of Clark Gable; plot complications break them apart and she goes to work in the circus, in a sleazy "exotic women" side show act, and in a quasi-brothel called the Paradise Cafe, while searching for "her man." Dorothy MacKaill, a New Orleans prostitute in love with a sailor, languishes in a tropical no-man's land awaiting his return.

Triumphs were fleeting; once the makers of the "fallen woman" films admitted to the impurity of their heroines, they felt compelled to dole out punishment with Old Testament severity. The admissions came quickly; the punishment filled the films. Mac-

Kaill is established immediately as a prostitute, Bankhead's virginity is soon lost to handsome Robert Montgomery, and Garbo has moved in with Gable before *Susan Lenox* is twenty minutes old. From these points on, the girls paid their debts to society; the depression setting made their catastrophic descents seem quite credible.

Yet a film like *Faithless* fancied itself spacious and broadminded. After Montgomery has taken Bankhead's most precious possession, he tells her, "You should be glad this is 1932 and not the prim 1880's." MGM press agents picked up this line of argument:

Could you stand the test? . . . Could you gamble your soul to save the love she held more precious than millions?
Will you call her sinner? What she did any woman might do.[3]

But this softening of the moral judgment is belied by the action of the films. Garbo, Dietrich, and Bankhead are forgiven by the men they love, while MacKaill goes to the gallows, yet this forgiveness has been permitted only after their lives have been gutted and their absolute dependence on men clearly demonstrated. When forced to rely on themselves, the heroines find that only their bodies are marketable. Each picture made evident the fact that no woman could perform work functions not directly related to sex. Once any fatal misstep occurred, complete ruin was certain, until a purification was effected which involved a virtual ceding of one's individuality for the love of the male. It was this dependence which Mae West would attempt to shatter.

The downward path of the girls was generally tied to the downward path of the society. We see Bankhead first as a spoiled rich girl, whose holdings evaporate in the Great Crash. She is forced to live off wealthy friends, and eventually to live with a wealthy nouveau riche who declares, "If it wasn't for this Depression, I wouldn't have a chance with a swell like you." The old social-sexual lines have been erased. When Bankhead leaves to find work, *Faithless* becomes a montage of rejections ("no help wanted—this means you,") and establishes the society's inability to provide work. Discovering her feminine incapacity to even feed and shelter herself,[4] Bankhead encounters the jobless Robert Montgomery—an advertising man likewise on the skids. They marry, he is beaten up by truck drivers when he tries to get a trucking job, and Bankhead takes to the streets. Despite her suffering this kind of degradation to keep him in food and medicine, the terms of *Faithless* insist that Montgomery forgive his wife at the end of the film. It is to his moral generosity that the dependent wife must plead.

Marlene Dietrich's role was similarly fashioned. As her husband languishes of radium poisoning, she becomes the mistress of a wealthy shyster politician (Cary Grant); he pays for the treatment. Her husband learns of this; Dietrich is cast out of the house. Without his love, she cannot function. She runs out of money, wanders to the South and is arrested for vagrancy, winding up in a New Orleans establishment which Von Sternberg made into a combination bordello and opium den. She descends even from this, to an all-girl flophouse overflowing with rejected and incompetent femininity. She finally becomes a mere name in the files of the bureau of missing persons.[5]

Marlene's last resort is her body. Somehow she sails to France, where she sleeps her way to the top and becomes the toast of the Parisian cabaret circuit. (Her means of progress recalls 1965's *Darling*, with Julie Christie utilizing sex to achieve celebrity. But Dietrich does so out of poverty and hunger, Christie out of boredom and anomie.) The experience only increases her devotion to a now-cured husband. She leaves Paris to offer herself, laden with guilt, to tame domesticity. Female dependency again carries the day.

The great Garbo was likewise forced to filter down the circles of hell Hollywood was dreaming up for women in 1931 and 1932. After being chased from her cohabitation with Clark Gable by a vengeful uncle, she joins a travelling circus (and sleeps with its owner), does a freakish side-show bit as demeaning as Dietrich's gorilla act, and lands in shyster city. Living with a crooked politician in a ritzy penthouse, she ultimately rejects it all to search for Gable. Garbo goes to the tropics and accepts employment in the Paradise Cafe, where floozies entertain sailors and men in Panama hats. Having made her commitment to one man and having erred, Garbo pays the full price, pinched and jostled in the Paradise Cafe. Genuine independence is never at issue. Not only is the Garbo (or Dietrich or Bankhead) character given no will to become independent, but the absence of any decent means to achieve economic self-sufficiency makes such a will irrelevant.

Bleakest of all, *Safe In Hell* started with the assumption that its heroine had no options other than prostitution or binding love. As a working prostitute, Dorothy MacKaill has transgressed the farthest and must pay the steepest price. Pursued by police in New Orleans she escapes to an extradition-free isle in the tropics, only to be trapped in the seediest of social worlds.

(It is noteworthy that Garbo starts in the northern plains and ends in the tropics, that Dietrich begins in New York and descends to New Orleans, that Bankhead leaves New York and moves in with a nouveau riche in Florida, that MacKaill moves southward from New Orleans to the tropics. Their geographic progress to warmer and more southerly climes invariably corresponds to a moral fall, and this is emphasized by MacKaill's presence in a "hell." That morality and latitude correspond is, by itself, not all that remarkable. What is significant is how accurately it demonstrates the really iron-clad moralism of the "fallen woman" pictures. The heavy symbolism of deflowered women sweating off their sins in fetid tropics gave away Hollywood's assumptions about sin and its price.)

MacKaill is the "only white girl" on the island. The other criminals sit around snapping at flies and lunging at her, and the film's pace—like a defective overhead fan—only deepens the atmosphere of ennui. MacKaill can do nothing about her fate, stuck in limbo. When she is given a choice between hanging and becoming the "sex slave" of the island's executioner, she chooses a melodramatic death. *Safe In Hell*'s unrelenting seaminess reflected the extent of the punishment Hollywood inflicted upon its "fallen women."

So women were left with a choice which was no choice at all: find one abiding love or perish. Movie heroines were in a really untenable position: the opportunities for sexual expression, identity, and a sense of individual potential were closed off. Until the finest woman who ever walked the streets started parading her blonde curls and creamy bosom across the screen in 1933.

WOMEN OF THE WORLD

Mae West

She was *the* sensation of 1933. Her second starring film, *I'm No Angel,* was, by one measurement, the greatest single box office attraction of the year.[6] Her first, *She Done Him Wrong,* featuring Mae as a belle of New York's saloon-oriented and male-dominated 1890s, had introduced the total West to Americans. The response was immediate: "Mae West sizzles across the screen and turns the town torrid," leered the manager of a Morris, Illinois, movie house, while another in Harrison, Arkansas, was "surprised that such a picture would be released by any production company," and the manager of Aurora, Missouri's Princess Theatre advised patrons to "tell the kids to come some other time."[7] She *was* rough. In *She Done Him Wrong,* she confides that the nude oil of her that graces a saloon "is a bit of a flash . . . but I wish you wouldn't hang it over the free lunch." "Come up and see me sometime" passed rapidly into the language and no Hollywood voice, except that of W. C. Fields, was more readily identifiable during the thirties. Her voice radiated irony, her eyes sized up potential lovers as though they were sides of beef, and her hips mesmerized a nation.

In the light of the pervasive and dreary moralism of the "fallen woman" films, Mae West laughed at sex and in doing so elevated the role of the woman. Gilbert Seldes' analysis was very much to the point:

Mae West's contribution to the treatment of sex on the screen is in effect the annihilation of two of the most famous feminine types in all literature: one is the seductress, the Circe whose love changes men into beasts; and . . . the delicate lady, shrinking from the advances of brutal men. In fact, her invitation "Come up and see me sometime" . . . suggests for the first time on screen that satisfaction will result from the encounter. She destroys the idea that women have no satisfaction in love.[8]

She made the female the hunter, not the hunted, an active participant in sex, rather than a passive and ill-starred victim. By asserting her faith in diamonds and baubles, she created the crudest kind of economic independence, but a woman with a safe full of jewelry would have to walk no streets. She could not be manipulated, refused to be solemn about her body and made it clear that she liked her pleasures and liked her freedom. She seemed in complete control of herself and her world. Hollywood convention married her off to people like Cary Grant, but her behavior throughout any given film let her audience know that no attachment was likely to be very long-termed.

What made Mae West really significant, and makes her films still a total delight to watch, was her sense that what had been labelled "bad" was only a human activity subject to all the joys, failures, and absurdities of all such activity. By making sex less awesome, she made its consequences and social reverberations less severe. A young girl has lost her virginity and tells Mae that now no man will take her. Her answer knocked out all the props of the "fallen woman" tradition: "When a girl goes wrong, men go right after her."

In *Faithless*, Robert Montgomery and Tallulah Bankhead start embracing; the next shot is the familiar Hollywood crudity of a clock advancing one hour. When we next see the couple, he hints that "it" has taken place in the interim. The talk is clouded, the act seemingly a function of time spent alone together and, of course, no good could come from it. Mae's sense of time and love was more spacious: "If you've got nothin' to do and plenty of time to do it in," come up and see her. "I like a man what takes his time," she sings. Such delight in the body aimed at exploding Hollywood sex from the deadliness of films like *Faithless*.

When Cary Grant asks Mae, "Haven't you ever met a man who could make you happy," her answer was liberating: "Sure. Lots of times."

If Mae did not exactly outline a model for feminine life styles in the thirties (for American women could not start toying with men and hoarding jewelry *en masse*), she made it very clear what women did not have to do and demolished the guilt-ridden terms of the "fallen woman" films. She had assertiveness and strength in excess; the West character was rich in ironic toughness, wit and sense of proportion, and these qualities helped unleash the screen female from her burdensome role.

The Sophistication of Ernst Lubitsch

Lubitsch habitually relied on European settings, and his perspective was always that of the jaded but spirited roue. He delighted in the gamesmanship of sex. Relations between men and women were not constructed of the cementlike bonds which made *Faithless* and *Susan Lenox* so ponderous. Lubitsch saw relationships as temporary and tenuous constructions, subject to constant variation. Where Mae West shored up the role of the female, Lubitsch managed to understand both male and female viewpoints, and to manipulate them.

A star director in Germany, Lubitsch came to the United States in 1923; by 1929, he was Paramount's biggest name.[9] In Germany, he had begun by directing historical dramas and turned to comedy, of which Siegfried Kracauer commented, "his comedies sprang from the same nihilism as his historical dramas. This tendency makes it easy for him to drain great events of their seriousness and realize comic potentialities in trifles." [10] His work for Paramount between 1932 and 1933 reflected a facile nihilism about personal relations. It was not the chaotic destructiveness of the Marxes, but for all the flip "sophistication" Lubitsch applied to the exteriors of his films, their comic energy and intent had that same corrosiveness.

Trouble In Paradise (1932), which Dwight MacDonald thought "as close to perfection as anything I have ever seen in the movies," [11] was a dazzling directorial performance. Lubitsch demonstrated a fluidity of movement which most talkies still failed to achieve; his camera never lingered unnecessarily and subtleties abounded. The story line involved a romance between two thieves (Herbert Marshall and Miriam Hopkins) who fall for each other

while plying their trade. She lifts his watch, he steals her garters
and they embrace. Lubitsch's sophistication about sex, and his
rebellion against Hollywood's monumentalization of illicit love,
also is demonstrated by his treatment of the protagonists' cohabitation: he makes no comment. They are obviously living together
(casually sipping their breakfast coffee) and they are just as obviously not married. It is taken as close to granted as it could be in
1932. (After the Production Code was strictly enforced in 1934,
such blithe sexuality would vanish from the screen.) Lubitsch con-
cocts an affair between Marshall and a rich widow (Kay Francis)
and makes his widow very much the cool seductress, sure of her
sexuality. (Did sexual assurance only come to the independently
wealthy? In this sense, Lubitsch stayed with the old standards—his
woman could afford her pleasures, freed from the economic consequences of sin.) At the center of all the relationships in *Trouble
In Paradise* was a fundamental cynicism. When Marshall leaves
Francis, he steals her pearls and their closing dialogue had all the
Lubitsch sheen.

> MARSHALL: It could have been lovely.
> FRANCIS: Glorious.
> MARSHALL: Divine.

It was all very posh and ultra-sophisticated and local theatre
owners figured *Trouble In Paradise* as "a picture for the class
trade" or "only [for] the classes." [12] At the end, Marshall and Hopkins rob each other and embrace: a love the basis of which is dishonesty, as was seemingly true of all relationships.

While Lubitsch's amorality and cynicism might have been anti-
dotal to the leaden moralism of the "fallen woman" cycle, the severity of his break was probably too great to be liberating, the jump
too great for the public to make it with him. But the director per-
severed. In a highly popular Maurice Chevalier musical entitled
One Hour With You (1932), he used his star to make adultery
charming. Alternately grinning and pouting, Chevalier spoke
directly to the audience and asked whether or not he should spend
the night with someone other than his wife. He decides it would

be a good idea, looks at the camera, and tells the viewers they would do the same. When he returns to his wife, there is no hint of moral condemnation or tearful reunion. He just comes home.

In *Design For Living* (1933), the film version of a successful Noel Coward play, Lubitsch was engaged in even more ambitious interpersonal games. He set Miriam Hopkins against two men: an artist (Gary Cooper) and a playwright (Fredric March), alternating their affections. She marries Cooper when March leaves town and spends the night with March when Cooper is traveling. At film's end, she decides to live with both, circumventing a choice which Lubitsch (and Coward) found irrelevant. Paramount's ad campaign made the Hopkins character into a kind of sexual New Deal: " 'Design For Living' sets a new code for women as Gilda finds her heart large enough to give employment to two boy friends." [13] "Code," "employment": Lubitsch had created an extension of the National Recovery Administration. A theatre manager in Stillwater, Oklahoma, endorsed the film as "something really new in pictures. Your patrons may not think so much of a girl who loves two men, but they will rave about the brilliant dialogue and masterful direction." Another, from McMinnville, Oregon, thought it "spicy; but no one will object." [14]

Lubitsch was extremely successful in countering the soap operas of the early thirties. His women were independent, "bohemian," and unawed by sex. As an indication of how permissive the early thirties could be, how quickly certain standards could be erased on screen and replaced by ones audiences would at least not revolt against, the Lubitsch saga, like that of the Marxes, is instructive. But Lubitsch's heroines took too much for granted to clarify the role of the woman in the thirties. Having assumed their sexuality and moved on to the more exotic pastures of adultery and *ménage à trois*, they left a great deal behind. If some audiences could bask in their sophistication, the life styles which paraded across Lubitsch's films could scarcely be helpful, or imitated.

And it is here that Mae West looms even larger. Her relentless search for good times was straightforward and nonexperimental: she took her men unmarried, one at a time. She did not take sex for granted, or take her audience beyond the very familiar. Sex was laughed at and brought in the open: continental sophistication had nothing to do with her success. The "strong, confident woman, always in command," emerged from her films, not from Lubitsch's brilliant directorial exercises. Her virtuoso vulgarity could easily link the joys of her body with a free lunch, yet it also lifted the woman to a stance of power. That power was sexual, but it also involved replacing passivity with activity as a way of relating to the world.

So many visions of women in a short time reflected some considerable uncertainty, an example of which appeared in *Scribner's* in early 1932. Mrs. Frances Woodward Prentice attempted to sum up what bothered her generation, and perfectly revealed the kinds of pressures women were feeling at the time:

I, who am 37 in this year of 1932, have fallen into a chronological air pocket. An air pocket inhabited by most of my female contemporaries. . . . In these days when it is smart to claim significance, we feel peculiarly without point.

We are trying breathlessly to straddle the tremendous gulf the war really did create; awkward Colossi, prevented from getting our feet planted either Then or Now . . . We were reared, educated, and married for one sort of life, and precipitated, before we had a chance to get our bearings, into another.

We are not very successful at being naughty. . . . Even our divorces are a bungle, for the most part. Perhaps we cannot take sex as lightly as the young, nor as calmly as the old.[15]

Such uncertainties were reflected in the widely varying roles Hollywood dreamed up for its women in the early years of the Depression. What were her limits? Her potentialities? And what would her society allow?

And beyond the role of the woman in a worried society lay that society itself. In the work of West, Lubitsch, the Marxes, and Fields lay signs that old verities, limits and definitions might be cracking apart. But by 1934 a line seemed drawn. *Duck Soup* could not hold Marx fans and the Production Code became a real force, cramping the styles of moviemakers. "However satisfying the Code might have been to the guardians of public morality," wrote Arthur Schlesinger, Jr., "it began the process of cutting the films off from the realities of American experience." [16] Worse, little that could be called liberating would come out of Hollywood again in the thirties. Success, law, social unity, federal benevolence, and social "concern"—these would be the ingredients of the fantasy America depicted for the rest of the decade.

5

A Musical Interlude

We're in the money,
We're in the money.
We've got a lot of what
It takes to get along.

We never see a headline
About a breadline
Today.*

Ginger Rogers sings this in *Gold Diggers of 1933*, as dozens of girls sing along, holding silver currency, giant coins, swaying and serpentining. This is a rehearsal for a new show, but the show never sees opening night because the bank closes it for nonpayment. Just when the girls are singing about never seeing a headline about a breadline, the sheriff walks in and tells everybody to get out of the theatre.

* "We're In the Money." Music and lyrics by Harry Warren and Al Dubin. Copyright 1933, Remick Music, Inc.

Then producer Ned Sparks gets the idea to put on a show about the Depression. Ruby Keeler and Aline MacMahon and Joan Blondell, hungry chorines all, give him the idea—and songs will be by the "poor" boy (actually a Boston blueblood with a yen for Broadway) who lives down the hall from the girls. They can hear him playing through the window and think he's great. He's Dick Powell!

> Come and see those dancing fee-eet.
> On the avenue I'm taking you to,
> Forty-second street.*

In *42nd Street,* the first of the big three Warner Brothers musicals of 1933 (the others being *Gold Diggers of 1933* and *Footlight Parade*), Ruby Keeler is just a chorus girl until Bebe Daniels, the star of the show, breaks her leg in a hotel room accident. With just hours remaining before the Broadway opening of "Pretty Lady," Ruby gets the part. She's coached by the director, Warner Baxter, who is a sick man but needs the money. He was the biggest director of the 1920s but the stock market crash wiped him out. Ruby does it all, learns the part in five hours, and becomes a big star, helped by Bebe Daniels who comes in on crutches and gives her needed encouragement.

Ragged Dick reborn? Rewarded not so much by hard work as by Fate—the man in the silk hat who will give Dick a job away from the shoeshine stand and the leg that breaks beneath Bebe Daniels? The same: Ruby was an Alger hero just as Rico was a Carnegie hero. And for the same reason: an audience which was starved for success stories, the older the better.

But do not belabor the musicals. If they were All-Success, they were just as surely All-Singing, All-Dancing and All-Talking, and they put Warner Brothers, paralyzed by Depression losses reaching 15 million in 1932, back in the money. Enough has already been written about their outrageous qualities: girls playing lighted violins, girls under water, girls playing big white pianos that kept

---

* "42nd Street." Music and lyrics by Harry Warren and Al Dubin. Copyright 1933, Remick Music, Inc.

moving around while they sang "In My Song Of Love" (in *Gold Diggers of 1935.*) Of course, they were escapist—a nation could drown its sorrows in legs and glitter, and plumes and teeth and sweet harmonizing. But the three musicals that made the most money, the three mentioned earlier, all had Depression motifs. Warner Baxter is broke in *42nd Street*, everybody is broke in *Gold Diggers of 1933* and star producer Jimmy Cagney on the skids ("Breadline, I hear you calling") in *Footlight Parade*.

Cagney is broke until he gets a fantastic idea. He will produce live musical prologues to precede the feature film! The audience, in tuxedos and evening gowns (and no movie audience wore less than formal wear to a musical prologue) will tell their friends. And this will make the prologues just the biggest thing in show business —and Cagney's reputation as a producer with it. He uses an example drawn from the business world, now apparently functioning in this last Warner musical of 1933, and says he will merchandise musical prologues in theatres like a chain operation, like a chain of drug stores, he says.

Many stores, same products; many theatres, same prologues, same songs and arrangements. The last song in *Footlight Parade* gives away Cagney's faith in business methods. When the girls do the big "Shanghai Lil" number (Ruby Keeler as Lil, producer Cagney himself—subbing for a sick star—doing the male lead), they hold up flash cards. One flash: the Blue Eagle of the National Recovery Administration. The next flash: a smiling and confident Franklin Delano Roosevelt. Roosevelt's grin informed Cagney's faith in the future. Roosevelt was a prologue, and even the Blue Eagle could do a number.

If *Footlight Parade* thought the business world and governmental world admirable, it might have had something to do with the success of its predecessors. Jack Warner claimed that *42nd Street* was a major factor in saving his ailing company: "The success of that picture was so sensational that it helped in no small measure to bring about a revival of general business and started it on the upgrade that it has been climbing ever since."[1] *Motion Picture Herald* listed *Gold Diggers* second and *42nd Street* third in its list of the top moneymakers of 1933.[2]

Later musicals were less successful. The big three of 1933 built their stories around backstage tales, had roots in misfortune, and cranked up the old success mechanisms once again. Later musicals groped for the forms that made the early three so popular. The opening of *Gold Diggers of 1935* was a pale imitation of "We're In The Money." Dick Powell, a singing insurance man, sings, "Just a little filthy lucre/Buys a lot of things," to a background shot of cascading coins. "We're In The Money," busted by a sheriff and deputies, was ironic. The point of "Filthy Lucre" was pretty hard to fathom. Was it satirical? It was not, but rather a mindless attempt to recapture the form of 1933s success without the spirit. *Gold Diggers* of 1935 and 1937 involved some mild spoofing of the lovable rich. *Gold Diggers of Paris* (1938) starred Rudy Vallee and had nothing, as far as one could see, to do with anything. Fred Astaire and Ginger Rogers, by their flip repartee and personal grace, were the last great practitioners of the art for the remainder of the decade; but the cast-of-thousands musicals underwent a lingering death.

The reasons were outlined by a theatre owner in Indiana:

I have only one complaint to make about the Gold Diggers series; not since 1933 has there been a worthwhile story. It seems to me that a series of this magnitude would have stories that appeal to everyone, stories that . . . are also human, down-to-earth, deeply interesting. There is nothing sincere or appealing about the story in this picture [*Gold Diggers of 1937*]. The ensembles are well done . . . but why expect musical numbers to hold up a weak, shallow, artificial story.[3]

The backstage musicals, in all their lavishness, were still related to facts of life in 1933. Their pointless successors were found to be a bore.

Part Two 1933–1939

6

Back to the Earth: King Kong and King Vidor

Kong is a triumph in trick photography but has little to offer besides that. A natural at the box office, with opinion here divided on its merits. . . . Don't let the patrons think it's another wild animal opus. Fay Wray and Bruce Cabot are very good, so play up the romance with the thrill angle. *And don't let them forget that the beast charges through New York City* [my italics].

—Roland Viner, Morris Theatre
Morris, Illinois [1]

They were not likely to, not with the poor gorilla clambering up hotel walls after Fay Wray, peering into windows with those quizzical, electric eyes. Not after he took a Manhattan "El" apart, holding blackened subway cars under his arms like loaves of bread, as the city-dwellers screamed and dropped out of the windows. And certainly not after he scaled the new (and, in 1933, half-empty) Empire State Building, gamely fighting off the airplanes as they circled to kill him.

The nation's ambivalent feelings toward her greatest metropolis (see Chapter 2), and its concern over social and economic chaos and incipient collapse, came out in *King Kong* and other films more explicitly in praise of the simple (and rural) life. It was popular culture's reflection of the "back to the earth" movement which had begun in the 1920s. As the Depression deepened (twelve million jobless at *King Kong*'s release), sentimental yearnings for a Jeffersonian life on the land became the basis for a potential "solution" to the nation's illness. By the time these yearnings got translated into legislation, the New Deal was setting up a program of subsistence homesteads for the jobless. Halfway houses between industry and agriculture, these small acreage plots were designed to attract those locked out of factories and farms. Among those administering the program were some who hoped for a slowdown, and even reversal, of the processes of industrialization and urbanization. That program would be a failure.[2]

Sentimentalizing the simple life was nothing new in American culture. As the cities expanded and multiplied in the late nineteenth century, America's large circulation magazines were filled with fiction and reportage about "wise Ohio mothers, old-timers with salty speech, farm boys and cowhands, kindly preachers and public school teachers, ethical corner grocers and blacksmiths." Their authors spoke "wistfully of the country and the old home town." [3] Through the 1920s and early 1930s, the joys of rural living were propounded by publisher and health faddist Bernarr McFadden, through his *Liberty Magazine* and scandal-laden New York *Evening Graphic*, and by Ralph Borsodi, whose 1933 *Flight From The Cities* made an early call for subsistence homesteads. In 1930, twelve Jeffersonian southerners, appalled by the quality of life in industrial America, put together a self-consciously reactionary credo entitled *I'll Take My Stand*. Their stance was rooted in the soil. Lyle K. Lanier's "The Philosophy Of Progress" declared that:

> . . . the large surplus of chronically unemployed should be induced by all possible means to return to agriculture. They would have a base on which to knit together the fragments of lives now broken on the wheel of what we are pleased to call civilization.[4]

Hollywood expressed this agrarian drive in a number of ways. Films in implicit or explicit celebration of rural life appeared: *State Fair, Our Daily Bread, The Life Of Jimmy Dolan, Stranger's Return,* and *King Kong.* And the kind of stars who brought people into theatres were not, as might be imagined, the glamorous and chic. As daily life worsened, people did not necessarily flock to see feather boas, creamy bosoms and platinum hair. The top five box office attractions of 1932 and 1933 were: Marie Dressler, Will Rogers, Janet Gaynor, Eddie Cantor, and Wallace Beery.[5]

Between 1931 and 1932, the third and fourth places had been occupied by Joan Crawford and Greta Garbo; a year later, Miss Crawford was tenth and Garbo not among the top fifteen. The most attractive stars of 1932 and 1933 were doughty, homespun, commonsensical and, with the exception of Eddie Cantor (who was homely and unabrasive, but out of an urban, Jewish, vaudeville milieu), not of the city. Marie Dressler, aging and soon to die of cancer, came on as everybody's favorite aunt: sharp-eyed, gruff but warmhearted. Will Rogers' immense popularity in the early thirties probably had less to do with his essentially gentle political "satire" than with his cracker barrel pose, that of the shy, head-scratching Oklahoman who grinned and kidded the Congress. His local banker in 1934's *David Harum* was a fount of epigrams, ill at ease in a tuxedo and most at home with horse-trading and small-town business values. When he assumed the role of the prize hog-raising farmer in *State Fair,* Dwight MacDonald was livid:

At a time when the American farmer is faced with ruin, when the whole Middle West is seething with bitterness and economic discontent, a movie like *State Fair* is an insulting "let 'em eat cake" gesture. The vaudeville rusticity of millionaire Will Rogers, the "cute" doll face of Janet Gaynor—thus Hollywood embodies the farmer.[6]

Yet however calculating Rogers' folksiness might have been, no male star attracted more patrons into movie houses.

Janet Gaynor was plain and sweet, the touchingly drab, small-town girl. When F. W. Murnau's silent classic *Sunrise* (1927) extolled the purity and decency of country people, she was the little farm wife, patiently waiting out her husband's flirtation with a city woman. Despite her own flirtation with a Des Moines newsman in *State Fair*, she unerringly returns to the farm.

Wallace Beery, while no farm type, had a directness and crusty hide more associated with the country than the city, or at least with the shyster city which was all moviegoers were permitted to see. With the ascendancy of Shirley Temple, the fact of America's search for some vanished innocence seemed confirmed. Shirley Temple's stardom and longings for the country were part of the same process: "back to the earth" was less a coherent plan for the future than a musing over things, imagined and real, that had been lost.

King Kong (RKO, 1933. Directors, Merian C. Cooper and Ernest B. Schoedsack)
The Life Of Jimmy Dolan (Warner, 1933. Director, Archie Mayo)
The Crowd (MGM, 1928. Director, King Vidor)
Our Daily Bread (United Artists, 1934. Director, King Vidor)

Films sympathetic to the simple life might set it against that of the shyster city (*Jimmy Dolan*), see it as curative of ills bred by that city (*Jimmy Dolan*), as curative of national ills (*Our Daily Bread*), or glory in it for its own sake (*State Fair*). Phil Stong's dismal novel, *State Fair* (published in 1932), "presented an Iowa family freed of all the provincialism of country hicks . . . secure in their love of rural life." [7] Dwight MacDonald, demanding a "realistic, documentary film of American farm life," saw in the film version of Stong's novel a "studied avoidance of anything more serious in the life of the farmer than whether the hog will win the state championship." [8]

Yet in the trapped and foreboding atmosphere of the early 1930s Hollywood could not bring itself to seal up its safety valve by realistically portraying economic conditions in rural America. The country was still Arcadia—an idyll, a way to escape the city and find oneself apart from all those shysters. Thus, Jimmy Dolan (Douglas Fairbanks, Jr.), an embittered prize fighter ("Nobody does anything for anybody else unless there's something in it; if he does, he's a sucker"), is forced to leave shyster city after a murder. He hops off a freight in Pleasant Valley and stays at a combination farm and orphanage run by Aline MacMahon and Loretta Young. Here his urban cynicism commences draining off, reel by reel, until he decides to stay in the country and live a decent life with Loretta Young. Since the shyster city was one myth and the country as an idyll was another, the film had little to do with anything in life except the outside chance that a simple, uncluttered existence remained a possibility. Since economics would have given the game away (why, in 1933, go to a farm?), the film did not stray too far from caricature. It was easy to leave a world of fixed fights, manipulation, and cheap blondes for one in which Loretta Young gently awakes you to milk the cow.

King Kong makes a reverse, and more epic, journey. While obviously no straight "back to the earth" saga, the film contains too many elements of both the shyster films and the rural idylls to be ignored in this context. The beast, do not forget, charges through New York City, and the people who torment him are lifted straight from the casting files used by the newspaper-lawyer-politico films. The entrepreneur who drags him from the land where he is "king" to the stage of a movie house, the arrogant and cynical audience which sits scoffing, and the newsmen who flash cameras at him were types totally identified with the city. Supreme in his own simple but rugged environment, the King is humbled by urban sharpers who are quite vocal about the process of degradation: "He has always been king of his world, but we'll teach him fear." Presented to the city on stage, his captor waves away the newsmen and tells the audience "He was king of his world. Now he comes as a captive, a curiosity for your eyes." Another sucker done in by Broadway.

So when the beast goes on his New York tear, the structures attacked, mounted, or disassembled are the obvious symbols of the city. Following a long interior shot of an elevated train, the straphangers dimly staring at their newspapers, King Kong caves in the tracks and superstructure. After he scales an apartment building, police and fire units combine to rout the creature who refuses to be a captive and curiosity. When he makes his way up the Empire State Building, he seems most heroic and most clearly trapped. Atop the ultimate emblem of the city, Kong represented, thought Bosley Crowther, "the gross power of primitive, emerging man. The modern man—civilization—calls forth the ultimate weapon to bring him down—airplanes." [9] But more so, Kong was an innocent of nature. "It was beauty killed the beast," mourns his captor, referring to the King's Andy Hardyish devotion to Fay Wray. The master of his jungle environment, the city literally enslaves him. What Roland Viner spoke of, sitting in Morris, Illinois, and reminding his patrons of Kong's rampage through the hated metropolis, suggests that people might have identified more with the King than they might like to admit. Kong's sad fight, a desperate and dumb creature captured and brutalized for a quick profit, does give him a strange dignity by the end of the picture.

But he was, after all, a gorilla. Humans got equally wounded. And no director dealt more sensitively with urban entrapment than King Vidor.

KING VIDOR AND "OUR DAILY BREAD"

Director King Vidor had been a giant at MGM in the 1920s. His story of World War I, *The Big Parade* (1925), was a huge artistic and financial success; his portrait of working people being mangled and damaged by the city, *The Crowd* (1928), remains one of America's great films. Surveying the nation in 1933, the director wanted to "corral this nationwide unrest and tragedy into a film. I wanted to take my two protagonists of *The Crowd* and follow them through the struggles of a typical young American couple in this most difficult period." [10] The result was *Our Daily Bread*, a very awkward and touching film about a cooperative farm. It was a simplistic movie but proved to be the only Depression film which genuinely felt that possibilities for alternative ways of life existed, and declined to parade the ethos of competition about the screen like an icon. Not surprisingly, Vidor had a very difficult time getting it produced and distributed.

The director wrote about the origins of *Our Daily Bread* in his autobiography: "I read a short article by a college professor in

Reader's Digest. It proposed the organization of cooperatives as a solution to the unemployment problem. He spoke of the possibilities of operating a farm on a cooperative basis." [11] That Vidor would be attracted to cooperatives and agriculture and see them as vehicles for the "John and Mary" protagonists of *The Crowd* was logical, for *The Crowd*, which Vidor hoped would have a "documentary flavor," depicted a city which had nothing to do with cooperation or community. It seemed a place likely to drive any sentient person back to the farm.

Vidor constructed no fake shyster metropolis in *The Crowd*. (The film was originally entitled *One Of The Mob* until MGM's "boy wonder" executive producer, Irving Thalberg, declared that "'Mob' sounds too much like a capital-labor conflict" and had it changed.) [12] His view of the city was seen through the eyes of "the average young man . . . Mr. Anyman." It was an entirely different vision than that of, say, F. W. Murnau, whose great film, *Sunrise* (1927) had a city all of flashing lights, painted women, and hot music. Vidor was not interested in depicting Babylon. His bad dreams were rooted in the profoundest of social problems.

John (James Murray—an unknown before and since) works in an office which now seems the cinematic realization of what C. Wright Mills would call "the enormous file" a quarter-century later.[13] He sits doing paper work at desk number 137 in a huge windowless room filled with row upon orderly row of desks, at which other hopeful young men in starched collars sit doing paper work. At five o'clock, the employees arise as one, to go out revolving doors and meet their girls. A "date" is no nightclub fantasy, but only more mass, organized activity. John and Mary (Eleanor Boardman—Mrs. Vidor) go to Coney Island, where the tinny japes and rides are enjoyed *en masse*. They go down slides in crowds and sneak some furtive sex in the tunnel of love, while more people wait outside to gawk at the couples necking as they emerge.

Marriage, Niagara Falls, and a grim wedding night follow quickly. John and Mary get a small apartment right next to the elevated line. They feel enclosed and bicker. But pregnancy "resolves" those conflicts. Even here Vidor scored telling points: his maternity ward was a metropolis of birth, scores of beds filling a room with the depth, height, and general aspect of a high-school gymnasium. A sensational image: infants delivered in quantity.

The baby arrives, but John still must confront the deadliness of his job. He feels stifled and yearns for his "ship to come in." Trapped in Algerish hopes for a windfall, he invents advertising slogans and mails them in, hoping one will prove to be his "main chance." At the film's opening, John is born. Holding him aloft, the family doctor declares, "There's a little man the world is going to hear from." It never does, and never will. The fact haunts him. Lost in the city, with nothing to cling to but a confused wife, similarly taken in by the windfall dream, he has nothing to live for but a myth.

It is not altogether surprising that John has a breakdown. Although his collapse is triggered by the death of his child, Vidor built it around his sense of impotence and facelessness. As the child lies dying after being struck by a car, John runs out into the street and tries to silence the autos, sirens, and newsboys, as though the noise of the city itself were killing his daughter. Afterwards, at work, John relives the death scene over and over, staring at the stacks of paper on his desk. Sitting in an office with a hundred other men, John is separated entirely from them. Speak to them? They are parts of a machine.

When he leaves his job, John is lost ("we don't know how big the crowd is . . . until we get out of step with it"), bereft of a wife who defines him as a loser within a system of winners. When John and Mary reunite, they go to a vaudeville show. John notices that the program contains the one advertising slogan, for a shoe polish, that he ever entered successfully. Rejoicing at this token of achievement in a perverse culture, he leans back to laugh at the show, and the camera begins drawing back to encompass more and more of the audience. Vidor's brilliant, crushing final shot shows the multitude roaring and thigh-slapping in unison, all together and all apart. "He had managed to find joy in the face of adversity," wrote Vidor. "A perfectly natural finish for the story of Mr. Anyman." [14]

It was not quite that simple, and *Our Daily Bread* indicated that Vidor knew it. The 1934 film opposed a cooperative life on the farm to an atomic existence in the city and set community against the hopeless, demeaning, and dehumanizing competition of *The Crowd*. John and Mary (now played by the wooden Tom Keene and Karen Morley, whose miserable performances contrasted sharply with the perfectly matched and delicate acting of Murray and Boardman), out of work, get the rights to an abandoned farm. Their ignorance of agriculture leads them to open the farm up to dispossessed passersby: first a Swede (John Qualen) and his family, whose possession-laden jalopy breaks down outside the farm, then a steady stream of unemployed and wandering workers. Vidor makes the cooperative farm into plain old American common sense: "If two men can do twice as much, ten men can do ten times as much."

Farmers, carpenters, masons, plumbers, a heavily accented tailor, bricklayers, even a concert violinist, all of varying nationalities, join the farm. A community of interests and shared experience is built: the land is held in common and everyone does the work with which he is happiest. Seen today, this portrait of the community—people living jauntily together in crudely put together homes—is awkward, uncharacteristic, and very moving. Especially moving today because that vision was never translated, during the thirties, into a real possibility for living. Even the stiff acting somehow increases the poignancy of people trying to build a community out of a tradition of competition. (One tableau: a brick mason is attempting to put together the wooden frame of a house, while a carpenter next door is botching the job of laying some stones. The exchange of functions is ritualistic: "I'm a carpenter," says the carpenter. They change places with much shaking of hands.)

Clumsy as it often was, *Our Daily Bread* was all about what Martin Buber had described as the true community; it was "a community of tribulation, and only because of that is it a community of spirit. . . . A community of faith exists when it is a community of work." [15] Buber would have had a difficult time in convincing MGM of the necessity for *Our Daily Bread*; so did Vidor.

Irving Thalberg would not touch his idea and neither would any other major studio. The director pluckily went ahead. "I was left with one alternative: to raise the money and make the picture my-self." [16] Banks were, needless to say, hostile. Not until Vidor had gotten the support of a financially sound risk like Charlie Chaplin could he get loans.

When the final product was released, it was jumped on by the Hearst press as "pinko." The Los Angeles *Times* refused to give *Our Daily Bread* advertising space and could congratulate itself later, when the film was awarded second prize at a Moscow film festival and cited by the League of Nations for its "contribu-tion to humanity." [17] Critical reaction in the United States was divided. The *Motion Picture Herald* saw "extraordinary topical showmanship values" in the film's scenes of drought: "the calam-ity has seared its effects upon mind and emotion." Therefore, stricken farmers would flock to the theatres! *The New York Times* thought it "momentous . . . the most significant cinema event of the year," while leftists were divided. *The Nation* thought it a "travesty . . . the familiar enough attempt of the liberal mind to reconcile the hope of a small collectivist unit with an acceptance of . . . capitalist society." *The New Masses*, however, hailed Vidor as a "Hollywood anarchist with an inherent sympathy for the underdog" while criticizing his "undeveloped political understand-ing." [18]

There was truth in it all. Vidor was no political heavyweight and there are scenes in *Our Daily Bread* with the depth and texture of a high-school pageant. When he stages a "political meeting" around a campfire, Vidor is so self-consciously American and commonsensical that he almost destroys the communitarian prem-ises of the film. The members of the community discuss future organization: one proposes socialism, another uses Fourth of July rhetoric in advocating republican organization (another complain-ing "that kind of talk got us here"), but finally the Swedish fore-man rises to scratch his head and declare "I don't know them fancy words, but we need a strong boss." All give assent as John is lifted to benevolent authority—the FDR of Arcadia. But the flaw is not vital: Tom Keene's pallid acting and the script totally negate his role as "strong man." Vidor had merely slipped into some sentimental, Capra-esque praise of people who knew no fancy words but had a job to get done.

"Getting the job done" in *Our Daily Bread* was the whole story. Political theory moved no one in an audience: ways of working, ways of living, these did. And for all the dumb show of the campfire meeting, *Our Daily Bread* was a subversive film, not for any attack on capitalism as such—*The Nation* was correct—but for demonstrating a way of life in most ways opposed to the tenets of American institutional life. The roots of sentimental longings for the land had been individualistic: Jefferson's dream of a republic of yeomen had been no communal fancy. Yet Vidor stressed the elimination of competition and the fulfillment of the individual in the group, rather than his submergence in the mass, as in *The Crowd*. Pioneer individualism had become, as his 1928 masterpiece tried to demonstrate, a dismal "competition" among automatons, pursuing the same prescribed goals. In *Our Daily Bread*'s lyrical, largely silent, final twenty minutes, the farmers, threatened by drought, build an irrigation ditch. Vidor's film comes brilliantly alive.

Vidor was concerned with life styles rather than economics, with cooperation as a way people related to each other rather than as a solution to the Depression, for it was hardly that. In the simplest terms, "bullies" and the covetous are thrown off the farm, yet those not "essential" to the working farm are gladly supported. While it appears patently absurd, and Hollywood fantasy, for an unemployed violinist to be taken on as a member of the community (giving lessons to the children of the others in exchange for food and shelter), it indicated the director's sympathies—how idyllic his vision of the true community.

Gone was the spirit of competition and entrepreneurial success which ran throughout thirties film. Vidor was proposing that people feel responsible to each other. Part of this was based on the kind of sentimental "good neighbor" ethic which ran through the films of Frank Capra (see Chapter 10). But more importantly, Vidor saw this responsibility as rooted in profoundly common interests, and saw that common interests and individual competition were mutually exclusive. Prevailing myths about life and work

made community impossible. *The Crowd* assumed that the social
and economic order had failed to create a humane society. *Our
Daily Bread* assumed that the competitive order had collapsed
and asked people to have goals beyond their own individual wind-
falls. "The real beginning of a community," wrote Buber, "is when
its members have a common relation to the center overriding all
other relations." [19] Individual fulfillment comes about, in *Our
Daily Bread*, because there is an overriding commitment—to the
building of a working farm and a human community in a seemingly paralyzed nation.

Where *Our Daily Bread* failed was in its refusal to recognize
the strength of the old ideals of individual success and competition.
"Most Americans," wrote Arthur Schlesinger, Jr., in discussing the
collapse of the New Deal resettlement program, "were children of
an individualistic and competitive culture, lacking any faith in the
community ideal." When the Subsistence Homestead Division of
the Department of Interior first envisioned the creation of farm
communities, with the inhabitants raising their own food and
doing their own woodworking and weaving, New Dealers were
greatly encouraged. The program's head, M. L. Wilson, saw "the
basis for a new type of civilization in America." Bernard Baruch,
Harry Hopkins, and Hugh Johnson all saw great possibilities for
the program; Eleanor Roosevelt was enthusiastic. "I can't help
thinking," said Secretary of Agriculture Henry Wallace, "that the
self-subsistence homesteads, if experimented with sufficiently . . .
will eventually lead us a long way toward a better world." [20]

But when the program was shifted to Rexford Tugwell's Resettlement Administration, it disintegrated. Tugwell ran twenty
resettled communities and plotted four greenbelt towns (greenbelt
towns being more rural, and more rationally ordered, forerunners
of suburbia), but the program lost momentum and fell apart. "The
aspirations could not have been more benevolent," writes Schlesinger, "but somehow, as [Marquis] Childs observed, the conspirators
neglected to take the American people into their confidence. The
whole effort skipped too many basic attitudes." "Cooperative"
was used as a scare word. When Muncie, Indiana's Council of
the Unemployed attempted, in March of 1933, to run some co-

operative gardens, the press declared it "the first attempt to apply socialistic principles to a relief program here." When the New Deal wanted to establish a subsistence homestead near Muncie, the "business control group . . . turned thumbs emphatically down . . . because of its socialistic features." [21] Alternative ways of life scarcely had a chance.

Vidor allowed *Our Daily Bread* to skip many of those deeply ingrained attitudes; it remained too much in the realm of fantasy to be truly educative. Most of the competitive tensions dissolve when the inhabitants reach the farm, as though it were a kind of Oz. When asked to throw their possessions on a common pile, they respond without hesitation. Tension grows in the community not because of competitiveness, but when drought leads its members to blame John for their problems. Dramatic conflicts which could have developed around the resentments of competitors asked to construct a community were instead wasted on bitterness against John and an outrageous, platinum floozy who wanders on to the premises and takes up with its "leader." The abysmal acting also hurt. By ignoring the opportunity to develop social conflicts, *Our Daily Bread* discarded its chance to have deep impact. So local reaction, when praiseworthy, hailed the film's timeliness in dealing with drought and complained of "too much footage digging the ditch," the scene most central to the message of cooperation. One who disliked the film declared flatly that "directors should not be social propagandists." [22]

Maybe not, but Vidor, with *The Crowd* and *Our Daily Bread*, had demonstrated practically alone (for there was Chaplin and *Modern Times* in 1936) how relatively simple films could touch upon the deepest dilemmas in American society. The trouble was that he *was* alone. *Our Daily Bread* was unique in expressing a need for escape from some unreal assumptions about life and work prevalent in an increasingly concentrated political and economic order. If the competitive urge ran too deep, the popular culture only reinforced it. If the New Deal community experiments foundered because of American individualism, it was because that "individualism" was not being redefined in relation to an ever more depersonalized and manipulative society. Who decided what an individual wanted, and how he wanted to live? *Our Daily Bread*, however crude, was one of a kind. Vidor had doubtless skipped too many steps, but if there was any time when Americans might have learned to throw some of their goods and aspirations on a common pile, it was at that juncture in their history when they had very little to give up, and their country and themselves to gain.

7

The G-Man and the Cowboy

Banished and mocked in the gang and shyster movies of the early thirties, the law made its movie comeback in 1935. Thick-headed law officers and shyster-ridden legal codes were subjected to changes of personnel and modes of operation. When inept police left the screen, they were replaced not by better police, but by an entirely different breed: G-Men. And simultaneously with the emergence of the federal lawman as hero came the re-emergence of the cowboy as a vital force in the movies. With actors like Jimmy Cagney and Edward G. Robinson playing agents of the Federal Bureau of Investigation, the law had a new vibrancy and toughness; it again became the focus of films, and was something to identify with. As for the westerns, their epic nature unleashed some powerful, if elderly, myths about the law as a great national, creative force. Between G-Men cleaning up the gangsters on a national scale and cowboys making the West a "fit place to raise a family," there really was little difference in intent. The law was again granted dynamism and the grace of its old associations, and could be seen as a benevolent national force. That these associations refurbished the image of federal law in 1935 and 1936, at the peak of the Rooseveltian consensus, is not so very surprising.

G-Men (Warner, 1935. Director, William Keighly)
Bullets Or Ballots (Warner, 1936. Director, William Keighly)
Public Enemy's Wife (Warner, 1936. Director, Nick Grinde)
The Plainsman (Paramount, 1936. Director, Cecil B. DeMille)
The Texas Rangers (Paramount, 1936. Director, King Vidor)

The establishment of law enforcement heroes was a careful and delicate procedure in 1935. Both the story line and publicity campaign for *G-Men*, starring Cagney, were case studies in Hollywood's trading in old myths for new. Very explicitly and in detail, the *G-Men* scenario was an attempt to make credible its hero's decision to join the FBI.

The industry was extremely conscious of its decision to breathe life back into the law. In the summer of 1935, as *G-Men* started playing dates around the country, Carl Milliken, secretary of the MPPDA, addressed the annual meeting of the International Association of Chiefs of Police. He claimed credit for Hollywood for a shift in public interest from gangsters to policemen:

We have passed a period . . . when the criminal seemingly held the stage. . . . By bringing the achievements of the police and federal crime detection agencies into sharp relief, the press and screen *reflect and foster* a renewed interest in the heroes of the law [my italics].[1]

The sense of Hollywood nurturing a renascent interest in the law was reinforced by Will Hays' 1936 MPPDA *President's Report*, which went out of its way to praise *G-Men* for introducing "a treatment which placed healthy and helpful emphasis on law enforcement." [2] The emphasis would "reflect and foster" a nation's regained health—an awakening from the delirious sleep of the early thirties.

Milliken had made a fairly politic distortion in addressing the police chiefs. The image of the local cop on the beat was only slightly improved in the mid-thirties; it was the FBI that found itself elevated to guardianship of the civic good. A scholarly study of American police published in 1936 observed "a general disrespect for the police on the part of the people. Thus there comes to be a sort of distastefulness associated with the police." And the Springfield (Mass.) *Republican* editorially hailed "the superior efficiency of the federal authorities as compared with the forty-eight sets of State and local authorities in fighting the outlaw class." [3] It was the federal law that drew the most favorable attention.

So it was that Warner Brothers, in its noisy attempt to canonize the G-Men, chose Jimmy Cagney to portray the heroic lawman. Cagney's passage to the right side of the law was treated by Warner press agents as an important national event. For what the switch represented, it was: a key step in legitimizing the automatic benevolence and righteousness of the federal government. " 'Public Enemy' Becomes Soldier of the Law," proclaimed the ad copy. "HOLLYWOOD'S MOST FAMOUS BAD MAN JOINS THE G-MEN AND HALTS THE MARCH OF CRIME . . . the fact that Jimmy Cagney, the historic 'Public Enemy' of 1931, now plays the lead in this epic of the end of gangdom, makes its appeal infallible." Not only that, the film would actually help end crime:

CAGNEY FILM ADDS TO GANGLAND PANIC

That Uncle Sam always gets his man . . . has long been acknowledged by the underworld, which for years has lived in mortal terror of the "G-Men"—the terms used to describe United States Federal Agents.

Now in the opinion of many authorities, First National Pictures has performed a patriotic service by showing how one branch of the government's law enforcement agencies will wipe out gangland.

Thoroughly aroused by the challenge of the underworld, the federal sleuths started out on a war of extermination.[4]

The early thirties had thrown in its guns, with a watchful and tough federal government making the appeal of the gangsters irrelevant and taking over their dynamics.

The story line of *G-Men* was constructed so as to make Cagney's character credible. He retains his gangland associations, having been put through law school (Phi Beta Kappa) by a racketeer who wants Cagney to shake off his slum background and go straight.

Cagney finds his legal practice failing "because I don't want to be a shyster," whereupon a law-school classmate who has joined the FBI urges Cagney to do the same. But his decision to join the FBI evolves out of the gangster values of loyalty and revenge. When the classmate is gunned down by mobsters, Cagney opts for the federal badge in order to avenge the murder. To make his conversion completely credible, he informs his hoodlum patron of the move. The old loyalties will not be strained: the mobster conveniently informs Cagney that he is leaving the business because "the rackets don't pay off, except in dough" (a statement that would have been completely incomprehensible in 1931). So his loyal and vengeful protege is freed to serve the federal government. With much shedding of blood, happily legitimized by his badge, he guns down gangland.

Details of plot showed *G-Men* to be steeped in early thirties motifs. When Cagney is almost dismissed from the FBI for his gangland associations, he carries the day by repeating his life story: Tommy Powers turned public defender. Referring to audience associations with *The Public Enemy*, the G-Man speaks of his child-of-the-gutter origins, boyhood scraps, and his turn to legitimate means of getting ahead via college and law school, the rise made possible by gangster financing. By buying the legal career of one of their own, the gangsters bring about their own elimination. In the context of early thirties film, it amounts to a near-ritual sacrifice. And more importantly, it represented a recognition by moviemakers that outlaws could not simply be banished from the screen. Their appeal had been too great for them not to participate in their own destruction in the mid-thirties. *G-Men's* real importance lay in the care taken to make credible not only Cagney's change in character, but the refocussing of emphasis on the ascension of a tough yet benevolent law.

The placing of firepower in federal hands represented another key detail of *G-Men*. A double hindrance to the FBI's effectiveness is revealed: G-Men are not allowed to carry guns and kidnapping is not a federal offense. Both wrongs are righted. Pistols are distributed to all the federal lawmen, and state lines, for the purpose of chasing kidnappers, are eliminated. The FBI and the government it serves are given the power and range to enforce the law on a national scale. Now its black sedans could do the chasing: the government could ride where it wanted, leaning out of the windows and firing away.

A Washington theatre owner played the association of law and government to the hilt. "When this was released we booked it for the Fourth [of July] and our hunch was a good one. We got the sheriff to arrange an exhibit for us. . . . Played to record weekend business." From Lamar, Missouri: "we honestly believe every theatre should play this for the reason that it leaves a lot of people thinking our government is okay." The veneration for the G-Men was not limited to moviegoers. In 1936, the House of Representatives voted to raise the FBI's budget from $5,000,000 to $6,025,000. However, the local policemen insisted that the FBI assumed credit for cases mainly fought by local lawmen and was too involved with glamorous and headline-catching manhunts. Senator Kenneth McKellar of Tennessee warned Senators against pampering federal lawmen.[5] But feeling, in 1936, was with the G-Men. By exorcising criminality and the need for illegal versions of the success formula, they helped legitimize the old delusions and demonstrate the dynamism of the federal government.

The G-Man theme was varied; in *Public Enemy's Wife*, Pat O'Brien proved lawmen could be lovers—winning the heart of, and socializing, the ex-moll of gangster Caesar Romero. Edward G. Robinson, in *Bullets Or Ballots*, did a fascinating mirror reverse of *Little Caesar*. A plainclothesman given a remote beat, he proves to be a double agent as he enters a gang from the bottom, works his way up, and destroys it. It was as if local lawmen had rented Little Caesar. "What makes it a good film," wrote a *Time* reviewer, "is that it brings Edward G. Robinson . . . back into the crime fold, this time on the side of the law." [6] As did Cagney, Robinson retained his old drive. Warner press copy quoted him as follows:

"A good detective should be a tough guy, too," says Edward G. Robinson, who has figured in many screen and stage melodramas working against the law, but who is expending his hard-boiled energies in behalf of justice in *Bullets Or Ballots*.

"There is just as much excitement in law enforcement as there is in racketeering. The activities of G-Men in recent months has proved that." [7]

It proved even more than that. Along with the renaissance of the western hero and the elevation of the federal government into a virtual leading man in Warner Brothers' topical films (see Chapter 8), it brought that law and that government into a strong position in the culture. The grim policeman of the early thirties had become an expansive but watchful guardian of everyone's interests. Hoodlums would turn craven at his approach, social problems would slink away like the villains of "Perils Of Pauline," and bad men would be driven from the West. If the New Deal could represent the "scientific crimestopping" of federal agents, it could also be an agent of civilization spreading benevolence from a white horse, driving the Indians from the plains.

SOME EPIC WESTERNS

As gangster heroes became the vital figures of the early thirties, cowboy heroes suffered a sharp loss in popularity. In early 1933, it was reported that the market for westerns was "rapidly declining" and production of the genre was being cut as much as 75 percent. A producer blamed "public taste . . . westerns have a more romantic atmosphere. The people are satiated with the old time, stereotyped, rubber-stamped horse opera." [8] It might have run deeper than satiation. That public would be loathe to watch civilization being staked on the frontier while it crumbled outside the theatre. If one wanted dynamism and gunplay, the gangsters provided it all, in a comprehensible and attractive frame.

The old western heroes either quit or drastically reshaped their images. Tom Mix announced that he was returning to the circus. Gary Cooper, 1929's Virginian, became a beer racketeer in 1931's *City Streets*. In 1933, western star Buck Jones found himself forced off the trail for the first time in his career, and reduced to Shyster City: "Jones appears in a role far removed from the corral and the wide open spaces, in a setting of skyscrapers and night clubs, in

'Child Of Manhattan.' " [9] The frontier had closed with a vengeance.

It opened again in the mid-thirties. Reports to the *Motion Picture Herald* indicated that studios in 1936 sensed a "growing appeal becoming evident from virtually all sections." Paramount began a cycle of epics—*The Texas Rangers, The Plainsman, The Texans* and *Wells Fargo*—while Gene Autry and Hopalong Cassidy rose in popularity during 1935. Warner Brothers announced the production of a half-dozen singing westerns.[10]

The Paramount epics in question (*The Plainsman* and *The Texas Rangers*) were epic not so much in a "cast-of-thousands" sense as in their self-consciousness about depicting History. In their concern with the coming of civilization to the West, they represented the mythic and expansive side of the mid-thirties legitimization of law and federal benevolence. Their themes revolved less around the individual moral dilemmas (and moral starkness) of a classic western like *The Virginian*, than around the growth of nationhood and justice. Gary Cooper's Virginian was obedient to a rigorous code which in itself brought civilization closer. In hanging his closest friend for cattle rustling, he not only demonstrates his purity of purpose but helps make the West a safe place for women and children. It is something his eastern bride-to-be cannot understand. Westerners, who live in these films with a constant self-consciousness about their roles as actors in a historical present, understand. They are all helping to make "new states . . . out of raw prairie land."

The epic westerns were less severe and were totally imbedded in themes of thirties film: the personification of evil, the saliency of corruption, the gang values of revenge, the emphasis on unified nationhood. Vidor's *The Texas Rangers* is a shocker, coming from so sensitive a moviemaker. Uncomfortable with myth, Vidor struggled through a hopeless attempt to make western types of Fred MacMurray, Lloyd Nolan, and Jack Oakie. Oakie and MacMurray are outlaws who join the Rangers as a lark. After gazing upon some Indian atrocities, they are socialized into defenders of the law. Their gangster values cause MacMurray to refuse to arrest his friend Nolan (as opposed to the Virginian's solemn lynching of his closest friend) and MacMurray to kill Nolan, after the latter has rubbed out Oakie.

Around these basic gangland premises was built a tale of the civilizing of the West and the cleansing of Texas. Vidor began with a kind of "March Of Time" narration over shots of roaming cowboys and cattle: "to insure prosperity and progress, the Texas Rangers were formed." The head Ranger (Edward Ellis) tells recruits that Texas Rangers die "for an ideal . . . so that Texas may be a civilized place." Civilization, progress, and prosperity lie just ahead—the perfect functioning of society hampered only by an "external" threat in the presence of red men. That "civilization" meant "prosperity" was made very clear when Ellis declares, after the Indians have been massacred, "Now that we've placed the Indians on the reservation, we can be prosperous." As always in the thirties, only external threats blocked prosperity.

When a final stumbling block to the conversion of "frontier into civilized land" is encountered, small wonder that it is corruption. Fred MacMurray is sent to clean up a town run by a corrupt boss and is warned "no gunplay, unless absolutely necessary." The shysters are, after all, white men. In exorcising external threats to national wealth and chasing after corruption, *The Texas Rangers* showed how time-bound it was. When topical films began dealing with national problems (see Chapter 8), the external threat was a constant, and institutional ills appeared nearly nonexistent. The series of shyster movies had been an extended metaphor for national uncertainty, substituting crooks for economic short-circuits, while the G-Men demonstrated the federal government's potency by chasing down bad men, the real public enemies. ("Beneath the enthusiasm for the war on crime," wrote Milton Mayer, "lay, after four years of national panic, the public's desperate need for a bogeyman.")[11]

The Plainsman was also intent on relating western myth to early thirties shysterism. A cast of legendary characters like Wild Bill Hickock (Gary Cooper), Buffalo Bill (James Ellison) and Calamity Jane (Jean Arthur) helps rid the West of Indians, but Hickock is ultimately done in by shysters who are supplying rifles to the Indians for a quick profit. Making the frontier safe for a national destiny, these great figures of the West are involved in a contradiction: committed to progress, yet children of nature.[12] But they are following the instructions of another mythic figure, Abraham Lincoln. He declares, early in the picture, "The frontier must be made safe," then excuses himself to go to the theatre!

Wild Bill feels uncomfortable in the new West, but feels compelled to bring it about. His sad, sentimentally played death bothered moviegoers, who wanted happy endings and living heroes.[13] What made his a typical thirties demise was that it was effected by shysters. What greater national criminal than he who impeded progress and prosperity by selling guns to red men. There were so many shysters to be eliminated and so many public enemies to be tracked down before the nation could function normally.

8

Warner Brothers Presents Social Consciousness

Around 1932, the brothers Warner began to address their studio to social problems. Throughout the thirties, the Warner studios produced a number of films which dealt explicitly with aspects of social and political life Hollywood usually shunned. Fascism and communism, picket lines and scabs, the New Deal and wandering hobo children all surfaced in the "topical" films. They remain, without exception, fascinating documents, demonstrating both a gritty feel for social realism and a total inability to give any coherent reasons for social difficulties. When they verged on indicting aspects of American society, the topicals would shy away and introduce conventions from the shyster films. With the exception of the pre-New Deal *I Am A Fugitive From A Chain Gang* (easily the best of this genre), the topical efforts reflected Jack Warner's abiding faith in the words and works of Franklin D. Roosevelt. Roosevelt became an invaluable plot device, a way to rescue the topicals from their own bleak implications, an unseen sheriff cleaning up the town. The federal government remained the hero, as in the G-Man cycle.

The topical films must be discussed in somewhat different terms than many of the other movies covered in this study. Never really major box office attractions (except for *I Am A Fugitive* . . . and *Cabin In The Cotton*—a study of sharecropping—which did well in 1932),[1] they cannot be adjudged as integral to popular affections and involvement as, for instance, the "screwball" comedies. But the topicals represented Hollywood's major attempt, in a period of social and economic upheaval, to assess and dramatize that upheaval. When topical films were successful and unified, as in *I Am A Fugitive* . . . , the result was a major document; when confused and uncertain, as in *Heroes For Sale*, the very chaos of plot and motive seemed to indicate how difficult it was for Americans to sort out their assumptions about the workings of society.

PRE-NEW DEAL DESPAIR

I Am A Fugitive From A Chain Gang (Warner, 1932. Director, Mervyn Leroy)

Mervyn Leroy's classic study of chain gang life was a transitional link from the prison film to the topical film. The motif of imprisonment and entrapment was a popular one in 1930 and 1931, and an entire cycle centering around prison life reached American screens in the post-Crash days: *The Big House* (1930), *Ladies Of The Big House* (1931), *20,000 Years In Sing Sing* (1930), and *Convict's Code* (1930), to name a few, in rapid succession. In the first three listed, a key plot line was that of the innocent man jailed and, in *20,000 Years* . . . , executed. Both *The Big House* and *Convict's Code* had large prison uprising scenes, and an edgy society reacted: the *Motion Picture Herald* predicted that the scenes "doubtless will result in the unsheathing of censor's shears."[2]

Leroy picked up on the persecution of innocents, but the means of entrapment he utilized reflected a social awareness, rather than the familiar plot device of the "frame up." *I Am A Fugitive* . . . was ostensibly an attack upon the chain gang system practiced in the South, but, despite the patent justice and necessity of that theme, its implications, in 1932, extended much further.

James Allen (Paul Muni) returns home after the World War intent on avoiding his old factory job and going into engineering. "I want to get away from routine," he tells his mother and brother, "and create." Family pressure forces him back into the drab security of the shoe factory. But the army has trained him to want better things out of life (a constant in American film), and he quits to search for a construction job. From New England to Louisiana, up to Oshkosh and back to St. Louis, Allen bums around looking for nonexistent work. Blank rejections pile up: Allen's sound and industrious energies are given no legitimate outlet. In St. Louis, broke and unshaven, he attempts to pawn his war medals and the pawnbroker opens a display case full of such medals. Fighting men returned to a losing, impossible battle in the United States. (This theme was reintroduced after another war, in William Wyler's *The Best Years Of Our Lives* in 1946, but as a selective and temporary injustice, rather than a symptom of social bankruptcy.)

Unable to cash in anywhere, Allen wanders about and is finally pushed beyond the pale in a dingy roadhouse. Already an outsider, he becomes an outlaw when a hobo companion suddenly waves a pistol at the counterman and forces Allen to empty the cash register. The law enters on cue and Allen is sentenced to ten years at hard labor. What Leroy had outlined in these gripping opening scenes was the process by which an individual could move outside the law by standing still. The forces that continually disrupt Allen's life are invisible but all-powerful: implied were a decaying economy and a rigid, depersonalized legal structure.

In the harsh and mindless world of the chain gang the imagery was all of confinement: the lock, the fence, the chain. And the camera lingered on prisoners' faces, all beaten in, devoid of hope or any sense of potentiality save the dull fears of beating and death. Black prisoners were segregated, and in an era when black people were depicted as having the emotional range of comic strip characters (on a continuum from "Lord have mercy" to a grinning "Yes, ma'am!"), Leroy presented them as suffering, trapped human beings. (In a contemporary chain gang exposé, Roland West's

Hell's Highway, the black prisoners could usually be found singing cheerful ditties.) Allen, who returned from the war intent on avoiding routine, finds his every move programmed and subject to the caprice of the sadistic guards. When breaking rocks, prisoners must ask permission to wipe their faces and relieve themselves; any independent action, or even motor movement or failure, is cause for whipping. Allen grows ever more desperate and escapes, bloodhounds baying at his heels. Having escaped, he becomes a hunted man, a life-long outrider, no matter how straight his subsequent behavior. So even as he spruces up, passes into society and assumes an upwardly mobile career, his success drive hangs under the same sword that dangled so suggestively over *Little Caesar*. For where death was the ultimate reward of Rico's success, Allen's legitimate, inside-the-law advances as an engineer must of necessity be on loan from a determined and unfair law. He goes to work for a Chicago engineering firm and from 1924 to 1929 works his way up, proving that success was solely a function of being permitted inside the system. He achieves a measure of prominence, but when an alcoholic floozy (Glenda Farrell) learns of his past and blackmails him into marriage, his security is threatened. It is destroyed in 1929 when Allen's wife, in a fit of rage, informs on him. Now an upstanding Chicagoan, his case becomes a *cause célèbre*.

A deal is made whereby Allen will serve a symbolic ninety days back on the chain gang, but he is leery, and justifiably so. No sooner is he back than the brutalization begins anew. After the ninety days have passed, the redneck prison commissioner refuses to effect his release. Near the breaking point, Allen escapes again, but this time into Depression America—with no job in sight. And so Allen, at picture's end, is a permanent fugitive, on the run, stumbling around the periphery of his paralyzed society. The film's conclusion is overpowering: sneaking home to say good-bye to his second wife, Allen's face is a sad, wild mask peering out of the darkness. "How do you live, Jim?" she asks. "I steal," says Jim, who disappears. For the second time, he has been forced outside the law.

Enmeshed in "crime" by his failure to find work, Allen becomes a social exile. Escaping in the 1920s, he receives a conditional success, a reward for his qualities of honesty and initiative. Dragged back into the chain gang, he re-emerges, after the Crash, into no illusory success, but only the lonely life-style of the petty outlaw. He has been mangled by forces he never really sees or touches.

The power of the film's conclusion was almost too much to bear. A theatre owner in Virginia complained that "the ending spoils this picture to a great extent," while another felt that "the ending left a bad taste." [3] A comparison with the ending of *Hell's Highway* is revealing. After a revolt of the chain gang, most of the prisoners are brought back. The Governor, a just man in a white suit, arrives to declare that conditions on the gang will be ameliorated. The prisoners seem pleased and the film winds up with some banter from a Mormon jailbird concerning the advantages of chain gang life to having three wives awaiting one's release. A mild chuckle, and all are glad to be back.

Between Allen's anomie and the chain gang as home lay no real distance. Both spoke to the paralysis of the world outside; neither related to a society of possibilities. In a sense, Allen's automatic mobility during his success idyll in the 1920s remains just that, an idyll. And its temporary existence in the life on screen dissipates like a mirage. One has not seen a bleaker film: it was the absolute nadir of hopes and possibilities as depicted in the movies. The national landscape seemed like an empty lot.

Confusion in 1933: The Topical Films of William Wellman

Heroes For Sale (Warner, 1933. Director, Wellman)
Wild Boys Of The Road (Warner, 1933. Director, Wellman)

The first topical film released in New Deal America was called *Heroes For Sale*. Jack Warner's closeness to the Democratic party and Franklin Roosevelt, according to a *New Masses* critic, was the reason Will Hays allowed his topical productions such political leeway,[4] and there was little doubt about Warner's sympathies. (The Roosevelt-Warner relationship was, in fact, a working one. *Mission To Moscow*, a sympathetic portrait of the Soviets released in 1943 and a cause of much embarrassment to the studio later on, was filmed at Roosevelt's request.) [5] The New Deal provided an instant resolution to the serious social difficulties raised by the topical films of 1933 and 1934, and the Blue Eagle of the National Recovery Administration frequently loomed in view, like an icon of social and economic harmony. If *I Am A Fugitive* . . . had been made in late 1933, the chances are good that James Allen would have encountered a sympathetic federal official at picture's end, with a just solution in sight.

But for all the magic lamp qualities of the New Deal's appearance in the Warner topicals, the films still reflected a good deal of turmoil and confusion. Central to all was doubt about the present and certainty about the past. In Paul Rotha and Richard Griffith's film history, the topicals were assessed as "negative."

They had no constructive programme. In reality, their critical attitude was hankering for the old days back, when work produced wealth, when there was room to breathe and a chance for everyone. They were a reflective and unconscious response to the despondency of a nation.[6]

The topicals *were* rooted in a longing for the old verities about work and success, but it seems pointless to blame them for lacking a "constructive programme." Films can help influence consciousness by depicting different life styles or by dramatically revealing social inequities. They can present radically different models of behavior with greater skill than they can possibly present anything like a "program." Even so, the topicals *did* propagandize social inequality and displacement and represented a conscious response to unrest and bewilderment. Their failure lay less in an ability to come up with practical solutions than in a refusal to confront the real depths of a crisis of confidence and an insistence on searching out personal evil as a source of social ills.

This refusal meant that despite their shakiness about the state of life in America, they never seemed to doubt either America's institutions or its institutionalized myths about work, competition, and success. *Heroes For Sale* was perhaps the most confused film of the 1930s for those very reasons. Embracing both turmoil and faith, the film turned anticapitalist, anticommunist, pro-individual initiative, antimachine. Watch it today and you sense how mercurial was the state of the nation in the first half of 1933, how receptive it seemed to just about anything, how desperate to get rid, once and for all, of a depression now four years old. *Heroes'* hero, again, is a returning veteran, Tom Holmes (Richard Barthelmess). Even before his discharge, he has been victimized twice: A bravery medal he deserved has been given instead to the cowardly son of a banker, and war injuries have led him into a morphine habit.

Holmes returns to the United States already manhandled by forces beyond his control. (Even the morphine was first administered by his German captors while he lay helpless.) As in *I Am A Fugitive*, which *Heroes For Sale* resembles greatly for about a half-hour, the protagonist is a victim, unable to fight that which victimizes him. Able to get work only at the bank owned by the coward's father, he embezzles funds to support his habit, is fired and committed to a "Narcotics Farm" for one year. He is released in 1922 and goes to Chicago in search of work.

Loretta Young gets Tom a job with a laundry. He rises apace and comes up with a "merchandising plan" which finds quick acceptance from the kindly owner of the firm. Work hard, think fast, and the powers that be will have to be impressed. If your boss is the right kind of boss. . . . The old model functions well for about a reel. A suggestive, if bizarre, subplot develops, however, and begins splintering the main plot line. Into the picture comes a Communist inventor named Hans, a kind of cartoon character.

An inventor: perhaps the archetypal American dreamer and man on the make. Name them—Franklin, Fulton, Eli Whitney, Carver and his peanut, the great Edison—and a dozen boyhood biographies come to mind. They were all models of achievement. A lonely and industrious figure, the inventor we read about as children worked late into the night toward the moment of discovery: a moment of social benefit and personal windfall. So a Communist inventor, working in America in the 1920s (and inventing factory devices to cut back on manpower!) was a screaming contradiction in images. The terms of his radicalism are plainly conditional, a function of his failure as an inventor. When Hans succeeds, his commitment to Marxism will evaporate, which is precisely what happens. He comes up with a laundry scheme and becomes the most avaricious of capitalists. Like everyone else, communists were simply waiting for the American Dream to blossom again.

When the invention is completed, Holmes invests and cajoles his fellow laundry workers into investing, meanwhile eliciting a promise from his benevolent boss not to fire anyone or cut wages as a result of the new mechanization. When the good owner dies, his successors prove to be bad capitalists, who immediately start wholesale firing. The employees are furious and turn against the machinery, not its owners. Against Holmes' urgings of reason, they storm the factory and battle with police. Holmes is unjustly arrested for a "heinous crime against organized society" and his wife is killed in the action.

Here the focus of the film seems completely muddled. Holmes' initiative and the profits that result from his ideas and Hans' invention reflect a faith in the Carnegie formula, as does the portrait of the old boss, open-minded and receptive to "new ideas." The riot against the machinery rather than the bosses is meant to demonstrate the workers' irrationality, while Holmes' arrest speaks to the injustice of the state. Simultaneously, the film condemns the greed of the new owners and makes Hans as ludicrous a capitalist as he was a communist. (While Holmes languishes in jail, the invention reaps huge fortunes and Hans realizes that "there is only one thing important in the world; to have money." Holmes wants his profits turned over to the jobless; Hans thinks the poor should be killed for the benefit of society.)

Heroes For Sale had faith in capitalism but none in capitalists. Beyond a nostalgic yearning for the benevolent profiteer, the film was nowhere, despite all its violence and turmoil. Having found something grotesque and mean-spirited in each class and ideology depicted, the film staggered to its conclusion with a heavy burden. It dropped this burden at the door of the White House, rang the bell and ran away.

When Holmes emerges from jail, he is literally chased from Chicago by "Red Squads," who have him pegged as a dangerous agitator. He must go bumming for work, having contributed all his profits to the establishment of a soupline. Holmes has good reason to despair, having been jailed, seen his wife killed, and finally run out of town for doing nothing but trying to become a mediator between capital and labor. Richard Watts, Jr., thought that "so great are his pessimism . . . and his distaste for capitalist oppression that there are moments when you suspect him of planning to be a sort of romantic combination of Somerset Maugham and Lenin." [7] And nowhere more so than in the conclusion of *Heroes For Sale*. But despite his miserably disheartening and embittering experiences, Holmes, marching with the jobless, voices his faith in "common horse sense."

"Did you read President Roosevelt's inaugural address?" asks Tom Holmes. "It takes more than one sock in the jaw to lay out 120 million people." And a closing shot highlights the soupline running on Holmes' royalties: the success of free enterprise feeding the wreckage of free enterprise. *Heroes'* ending represented what theology recognized as the "leap of faith," the point at which system ended and heart began. Holmes' faith is greatest when his nation is at its worst. *Heroes* commits itself to formless good will by embracing Roosevelt's stout-hearted rhetoric and ducking all the questions it raised earlier: How did worker cope with machine? Did being a capitalist entail malevolence or benevolence, or were these categories relevant at all? What about those Red Squads, whom did they serve? The blanket answer, "common horse sense," meant only a closing invocation to the renewed liberation of individual initiative. The Holmeses of the world must be freed to build better laundromats, and become industrial diplomats. As Richard Watts, Jr., sadly observed, "what might have been a courageous picture ends by seeming just another futile essay in liberalism." [8] Handled gingerly by the trade papers ("more than usual care should be exercised in handling this. In many locales . . . it may be dangerous."),[9] the film quickly faded into oblivion.

In his next effort to be topical Wellman used more coherent material. *Wild Boys Of The Road* was a relatively simple story of high school kids forced to ride the rails when their parents get thrown out of work. Where *Heroes* was confused but ultimately

simple-minded, *Wild Boys* made its political naïvete less noticeable
by reducing the complexity of its theme. A major difference was
Wild Boys' obvious sympathy for the teenagers' use of violence
when necessary. Perhaps because they *were* children and would,
of course, grow out of it.

One could sympathize when the adolescents resorted to force
because Wellman was careful to show how typical they really were,
living in that Hollywood small town of white picket fences, jalopies, and high school dances. The innocence and seeming stability of that world is shattered when their parents are thrown out
of work. The protagonists (Frankie Darro and Edwin Phillips) go
bumming on freights, hoping to find work. They find instead hundreds of similarly displaced youths.[10] When a railroad official forces
all of them off a train, an old-time hobo advocates force: "You're
an army, ain't you?" They take his advice and severely beat the
official. Ends justifying means? Perhaps, but their action is revealed
to be less a revolt against property and authority than a struggle
of good versus evil: we learn that the railroad man has raped young
Rochelle Hudson in a freight car.

The youths' other struggle against authority is also qualified
They arrive in Cleveland and establish a "sewer city" in which
to live. When the police arrive to remove them gently, the teenagers react by stoning them, entrancing *The Nation's* William
Troy: "Never before does one recall an American picture whose
climax is . . . a pitched battle between a band of ragged outlaws
and the police, in which the sympathy is manifestly with the former."[11] Yet this moment of revolt was finessed into near meaninglessness. If the railroad official was a molester of teenagers, the
forces of civic order are clearly family men. When firemen are
called upon to turn their hoses on the "sewer city" occupants, one
declares, "This is a rotten trick." His colleague replies, "How do
you think I feel, with two kids of my own." We have been nicely
set up for the ending of *Wild Boys*: the triumph of benevolent
authority. The kids are in the right and no one is in the wrong,
except for the unseen social dislocation which has rendered their
families penniless.

When Darro and his friends arrive in New York, they set up

housekeeping in a garbage dump. Darro is used by some thieves and stumbles into arrest. The youth is not just placed into limbo, as in *I Am A Fugitive* . . . , but comes up before a judge with a Blue Eagle on the wall. The judge (Robert Barrat) wears rimless spectacles and is a reasonable facsimile of the President of the United States.[12] He listens with assured compassion to Darro's brief on behalf of underprivileged children: "jail can't be any worse than the street." Barrat nods knowingly and intones, "Things are going to get better all over the country. . . . I know your father will be going back to work soon." And so all the battling, rock-throwing, and hassling with authority is no metaphor; just the depiction of a justifiable grievance being resolved by a wise and silver-haired government.

William Troy refused to swallow the ending to *Wild Boys*, with its ritualistic invocation of the great Blue Eagle: "What we take away from this picture," he wrote in *The Nation*, "is not so much the renewed hope that this symbol [the Blue Eagle] should evoke as the feeling that our society is simply deluding itself if it pretends not to hear the barbarians at the gates." [13] Maybe. But if *The Nation* saw *Wild Boys* as the possible overture to apocalypse, the *Motion Picture Herald* sold the film to exhibitors as a kind of memoir of the bad old days. The *Herald* was not completely obtuse to socio-political facts of life. In May of 1933, it had urged "more than usual care" in the promotion of *Heroes For Sale*. "In many locales, due to mob scenes," it warned, "it may be dangerous." [14] But the frame of reference used in describing *Wild Boys* was drastically different. A degree of the edge was off.

Although the theme of First National's "Wild Boys Of The Road" undertakes to present a sociological and economic condition which to an extent has passed from the popular mind, it is still sufficiently timely to offer excellent opportunities to the exhibitor. It can be made particularly effective with a selling reference to the New Deal arrangement of the Civilian Conservation Corps, serving to take thousands of young men from the streets and freight cars. In many cases, the picture may strike directly home to the community, a thought not to be overlooked by the showman.[15]

Besides the assumption that the desperate world of *Wild Boys* was no longer salient to the "popular mind," the assurance of this analysis, compared to the jittery warnings about *Heroes*, is remarkable. What had been potentially dangerous about *Heroes* in May became a selling point for *Wild Boys* in September: its relevance to the community. *Heroes* saw instability all through the society and was dubious about all shades of ideology. *Wild Boys* sympathized with the plight of the young but radiated a greater amiability than any previous topical film. The uneasiness that could produce a clearly partisan fight between young people and police had obviously not vanished, but the social evil that had engulfed *I Am A Fugitive* . . . and mangled the story line of *Heroes* was being isolated.

This isolation was completed in *Massacre* (1934), *Black Fury* (1935), and *Black Legion* (1936), and entailed two trends: the reduction of complex social ills to instances of personal evil and a real ambivalence about the intelligence, decency, and stability of the lower and lower-middle classes. These were not so much new factors as enlargements and rearrangements of the old ones. The sadistic prison personnel of *I Am A Fugitive* . . . , the bad capitalists of *Heroes*, and the lecherous railroad official of *Wild Boys* were all in the tradition of movie heavies. But these figures competed with forces that were invisible yet shaped the development of all the films: the order that would not hire James Allen, the society that made Holmes a drug addict, "Red agitator," and jobless drifter, and the society that forced the wild boys out on the road. What in the society caused these awful and dispiriting circumstances was not spelled out. It was just there.

In the second half of the decade, the unseen became visible and was revealed to be nothing but the old shyster mechanism cranked up again. Bad men pulled the strings. The disturbing new trend involved the ease with which these shysters fastened on, and encouraged, working class discontent. This discontent, magically kept free of economics, was perceived as a threat to democracy. The second trend was not present in *Massacre* but powerfully evident in *Black Fury* and *Black Legion*.

Massacre (Warner, 1934. Director, Alan Crosland)
Black Fury (Warner, 1935. Director, Michael Curtiz)
Black Legion (Warner, 1936. Director, Archie Mayo)

Massacre was appalled at the treatment of Indians, and forthrightly laid the blame on the sadistic shysters in charge of reservations. The film was transitional in largely completing the transfer of social evil to personal evil, leaving just a few doubts not exchanged for New Deal assurances.

Its protagonist, Thunder Horse (Richard Barthlemess), is in the throes of an identity crisis when he returns to his old reservation. He works at the Chicago Century of Progress in a Wild West Act, riding around and whooping it up. Thunder Horse finally takes off his fake braids and says, "I'm getting pretty stale at this Indian business." He returns to the reservation to visit his dying father, only to be treated as second-class material by the ruling coalition of corrupt government agents and white merchants. The discrimination forces him to embrace his Indian identity. The injustice is the responsibility of the federal government, but the wrong one, not the new one. The old government is personified in the form of incredibly dishonest and rotten agents. One is Sidney Toler (an actor who would soon assume the Oriental guise of detective Charlie Chan). Toler has a final screen fling as a white man and rapes Thunder Horse's kid sister, as the other agents yawn and look away. As one commentator noted, "It does seem unlikely that *all* the white Indian Affairs Officers were corrupt thieves, lechers and drug addicts." [16]

Thunder Horse gets revenge and kills Toler, is arrested and convicted by a kangaroo court on the reservation. He breaks out of jail and heads straight to Washington (the audience being treated to an opening shot of the Capitol dome seen over a fence on which was stamped the Blue Eagle—instant affirmation). There he meets the New Deal Indian Commissioner, who is extremely understanding and courageous. He warns Thunder Horse that "the most powerful interests in the country will try to smash you, but they'll have to smash me first." Who these interests are, and why, in 1934, they place such weight on the continued suppression of Indians, is not clear. But the line represented a species of vague doubt which, many times amplified, pervaded the earlier topical films. Thunder Horse is brought back for trial as the Indians revolt and burn down the courthouse, but their leader opts for a government: working for the New Deal is "a real job."

The New Masses bitterly observed that "the Great Father Roosevelt . . . solved for the first the American Indians' problem," [17] and was not far removed from the real tone of this film. But at least Massacre demonstrated a genuine indignation at the shoddiness of the red man's role in a country he had once roamed unimpeded. Not all of its rage and concern was directed at shysterism.

By the time Black Fury was made, social reality was being bypassed in favor of a confrontation between shysters and the New Deal as ritualized as Kabuki drama.

Black Fury was one of the real frauds of the thirties, a fact recognized by many contemporaries. Not that it did not get some auspicious notices: New York's Democratic Senator Robert F. Wagner thought it a "vivid portrayal of a coal mine strike" and John L. Lewis, "a great contribution to the comprehension of the deepseated problem involved in industrial relationships." [18] The New Republic hailed it as "the most powerful strike picture that has yet been made," while New York's censor board threatened to cut its "inflammatory scenes." [19]

The object of this adulation and fear was a film about a goodnatured Polish miner who is manipulated by a shyster detective agency into leading a Pennsylvania wildcat strike. Black Fury had all the trappings of a proletarian drama: the realistic coal town setting, the working class camaraderie, and the brutality of industrial police. Yet it was simply a fairy tale, weighed down by shyster motifs and sure of the intrinsic solidarity between benevolent capitalism and conservative unionism. In its basic assumptions of social unity, Black Fury had more ties to "screwball" comedy (see Chapter 10) than to earlier topical films.

Its protagonist, Joe Radek (Paul Muni) is the epitome of the good worker. Popular with the other miners, he boasts, "Joe Radek like everyone and everyone like Joe Radek." His basic philosophy is popular with the mine-owners: "work like a mule." A fellow miner, who is in reality employed by a detective agency which feeds off labor trouble, sees Radek as the perfect dupe to lead a wildcat strike and necessitate the hiring of strikebreakers and detectives. Furthermore, Joe's class-consciousness is minimal. He will mine only until he has the capital to purchase a farm. It is therefore not surprising that events only indirectly connected to social injustice make him play a role in the action: his girl friend runs off with a company cop.

In setting up its labor confrontation, *Black Fury* raises some real problems and then proceeds to pretend that they are hallucinatory. Dissident miners complain that their leadership is stodgy and stale, collecting big salaries, and selling out their interests by promising the mine-owners no labor difficulties. The film embraced the premises of the shyster films by ascribing this discontent entirely to manipulation by the crooked strikebreaking agency, which needs conflict to remain in business. If assaults upon established trade union leadership had to be engineered entirely by shysters, then the fabric of industrial relationships must be sound, so long as corruption could be combatted. Small wonder that John L. Lewis found *Black Fury* so compelling a document.

Once the premises have been so thoroughly falsified, the film's "realism" seems an irrelevancy. With his woman gone, Radek is shattered and easily persuaded to lead a wildcat strike. The benevolent mine-owners reluctantly call in scabs and request the detective agency to refrain from violence. As the strike continues, wildcatting workers get evicted from their homes and go hungry. But no unsettling and impenetrable social malfunction is at work; the villains have been marked and labelled.

The question of police violence is dealt with frankly, but it seems honest only if one forgets the convoluted plot line. Industrial policemen, many of them depicted as obvious thugs just recently garbed in the finery of law enforcement, kill a friend of Radek's. The death incites him into dramatic action. Determined to have the company withdraw its scabs, Joe sneaks into the mine and sets off explosives, threatening total destruction unless his demands are met. It is a tense moment. The confrontation dissolves, however, as the New Deal rides into town. The appearance of the federal government sets everything right: the maneuverings of the detective agency are revealed, and confusion and ill-will vanish.

Black Fury's fundamental dishonesty was perceived by all kinds of critics. *New Masses'* reviewer Peter Ellis insisted that the film was "a calculated attack upon the rank and file movement" and accurately added that it was "so constructed as further to confuse millions of workers who are already confused about the real social and political issues of today." Andre Sennewald, of *The New York Times*, blasted it as "a handsome defense for the status quo." *Black Fury* "hints that once the bad old racketeers have been jailed, the workers and the operators resume their cordial labor-capital entente." And even *The Literary Digest* accused the movie-makers of "oversimplification" and felt it "too cautious to be . . . properly striking or important." [20]

The shyster as prime mover appeared again in *Black Legion*, yet this study of incipient vigilante nativism was a vastly more honest and disturbing film than *Black Fury*. It manifested powerful doubts about members of the lower middle class and made it clear that the nation had no shortage of human resources for hysteria, big-otry, and night-riding violence. Like *Black Fury*, it had no doubts that working people were the most likely dupes in the population. Its central figure, Frank Taylor, was played by Humphrey Bogart as a neurotic lowbrow, all suspicion and "de's" and "dem's." He was the factory hand as threat—the possible flaw in the democratic structure. Badgered by everyone, desirous of success, he is turned against foreigners when his success dreams turn sour. Since any American who applied himself was within reach of his most cherished goals, Frank has no one to blame but himself. Shysters feed on his frustration.

At first, he seems a happy-go-lucky family man; *Black Legion* deepened its impact by picturing Taylor as the guy next door. (This was slightly undercut by the fact that nearly all the char-acters Bogart played during the thirties teetered on insanity: Duke Mantee in *The Petrified Forest*, Babyface Nelson in *Dead End*, plus a dozen other gangsters or John Doe parts. That haunted look that flickered in his eyes when crossed, those tics around the mouth, marked most of his characterizations up to *The Maltese Falcon*.) Taylor sails home confident of an imminent promotion to foreman at the plant and has plans for a new car: "I got the swellest wife and kid in de world and the best ain't too good for em." His hopes for advancement crumble when the job is given to a Pole, one Joe Dombrowski. Coming home embittered, Frank turns on his large console radio and hears an agitated voice calling for "America for Americans" and urging fellow purebloods to keep foreigners from taking jobs meant for the natural of birth. Frank vigorously agrees. He is, at this point, only one more surly and frustrated citizen.

At work, Taylor is given orders by the hated Dombrowski, and grows angrier, goaded by a co-worker who asks, "How does it feel to get pushed around by a Hunyak?" It feels none too good, and Frank is easily talked into attending a meeting of citizens concerned about the foreign menace. The cell-like meeting, held in the back of a local drug store, is attended by petty merchants and factory hands. Impressed by the nativist speeches, Frank joins up.

The Black Legion is a Ku-Kluxish organization, replete with hoods, robes, and ritualized initiation. But at the initiation ceremonies, with a lot of scary and hysterical pledge-reading, *Black Legion* first begs the question. Frank is told that he must purchase a fifteen-dollar revolver and a six-dollar uniform; when he hesitates, a Legion superior bullies him into paying up. Apparently, someone is in vigilante-ism for profit, and we are shortly introduced to that someone. A kinsman of *Black Fury*'s head strikebreaker, the organizer of the Legion is yet another in Hollywood's endless storehouse of shysters, an apolitical sharper who aims to set up his burgeoning organization on a nationwide basis, getting wealthy from dues and gun sales.

This irrelevant corruption is not quite so damaging to *Black Legion* as it was to the plot of *Black Fury*. It cripples the impact of the film in that it ascribes the genesis of this nativist vigilante-ism to the opportunism of a simple hustler. But the film does not shrink from depicting the wealth of raw material and barely repressed violence for such a movement. In the reels preceding and following the introduction of the Legion's shyster director, the real ugliness of his followers is demonstrated: running Dombrowski out of town, burning down his father's farm, flogging an Irishman, destroying foreign-owned stores. It was the first Warner topical film that looked toward the ethos America would bring to World War

Two—one that stressed social unity and insisted that prejudice was an affront to the American standard of fair play. Postwar films about returning veterans invariably used bigotry as a key justification for America's presence in the war.

But *Black Legion* was enough of a Depression film to stress how bigotry affected one's success drive. Having gotten his promotion after the disappearance of Dombrowski, rather than through his own initiative, Taylor has short-circuited the success model. He will pay for it, and thus loses his promotion by the means that achieved it: the Legion. Sloughing off from work to proselytize for the movement, Taylor seeks recruits while a machine breaks down unattended. He is blamed and demoted. This done, the rest is predictable: it is Carnegie run backward. Frank's undemocratic behavior causes his work to suffer and he loses his promotion. He drinks, beats his wife, and shoots his best friend when the friend suspects his connection to the Legion. Jolted into reality by this act, Frank is arrested and informs on the Legion. All its members get life imprisonment.

While it lacked the overpowering impact of *I Am A Fugitive . . .* , *Black Legion* was a strong film, and part of that strength lay in its refusal to wheel in the federal government as a *deus ex machina*. It had faith in its audience's ability to focus its righteousness without the New Deal audio-visual aids. But its evasions were its evasions. Like all the topicals after *I Am A Fugitive . . .* , it was too concerned with finding fall guys for social dislocation and turmoil. It feared the volatility of working classes, but defined that volatility in terms of lynching, vigilante-ism, and manipulation by shysters. A benevolent government would have to be watchful of its citizenry.

I Am A Fugitive . . . and *Black Legion* were produced a mere four years apart, yet the distance between them seems immense: it was the distance between desperation and "concern." It was the distance between a society that seemed utterly devoid of potential and a society that could occupy itself with the defense of democratic prerogatives.

9

The Mob and the Search for Authority, 1933–1937

If the "back to the earth" movies were an essentially sentimental response to the Depression, and if the topical films responded by converting serious disorders into simple conflicts of bad guys and good federal government, a third response contained some wilder, and more appalling, possibilities. In 1933 and 1934, a cycle appeared that appealed to a craving for authority and argued that the nicer points of means be disregarded for some decisive ends. The progression went from praise of mob action (*This Day And Age*) to advocacy of an American dictatorship (*Gabriel Over The White House*) to the healing grace of a paternal, quasi-constitutional leader modelled upon Franklin Roosevelt (*The President Vanishes*). The movement and orientation of these three films went from crowd on up—to a leader who would blast open mob frustrations over the dreary condition of American life in 1933. By the middle of the decade, Hollywood started arguing from the top down: speaking from assumed federal benevolence to the instability of the crowd. The result was two intriguing films

about lynching and mob rule—*Fury* and *They Won't Forget*—
which amply demonstrated how the assumptions of 1937 differed
from those of 1933.

This Day And Age (Paramount, 1933. Director, Cecil B. DeMille)
Gabriel Over The White House (MGM, 1933. Director, Gregory
  LaCava)
The President Vanishes (Paramount, 1934. Director, William
  Wellman)

From 1932 to 1935, the possibility that a homegrown fascist
government could spring forth in the United States was open for
general debate. Hitler's Germany seemed galvanized, Mussolini
made the trains run *allegro con brio*, and some sophisticated com-
mentators saw in the National Recovery Administration the seeds
of an American corporate state. In the middle of 1932, with panic
deepening, Pennsylvania's Senator David Reed declared that "if
ever this country needed a Mussolini, it needs one now." [1] Homegrown figures on the far right ranged from calm respectability to
full-blooded lunacy, from authoring books for eminent New York
publishers to meeting in piney woods under full moons. Harvard-
educated Lawrence Dennis composed deliberate and sober tomes
advocating fascist organization, while William Dudley Pelley was
called upon by God and the zodiac to form the Silver Shirts in
Asheville, North Carolina. [2] When Father Charles Coughlin and
Huey Long (whose dictatorial tendencies are increasingly in question) [3] crested in popularity between 1934 and 1935, Sinclair Lewis
was compelled to envision in *It Can't Happen Here* an America
whose politics were an organized violence, secret police and concentration camps, the sure ends of a nation's search for authority.

While the right-wing threat, in its organized state, appeared
most severe (and gave Franklin Roosevelt's political advisors their
most troubled hours) in 1935, Hollywood's year to conjure up
exotic political visions was 1933. Films of this political genre were
not so much specifically fascistic as they were deeply authori-
tarian, reacting to what Arthur Schlesinger, Jr., saw distinguishing
America's winter of 1932–1933: "a cult of direct action." [4] The
rhetoric and imagery utilized looked not only to what Lewis would

react against in *It Can't Happen Here,* but to the symbolism of
the Nazis.

If this last observation seems hysterical, let us examine three very
disparate cultural documents, in connection with Cecil B. DeMille's
This Day and Age, a film which praised high school students
for taking the law into their own hands and that showed nothing
but contempt for the due process of law. The students were shown
as typical blonde specimens of American innocence, cheerily enmeshed in a world of dating and jalopies, and then made to effect
a near-lynching, torches blazing. The result, viewed today, is unsettling and perverse: too many cultural and historical images
conflict. Imagine Josef Goebbels writing "Meet Corliss Archer."
But the documents tell all.

1. 5000 stalwart youths . . . determined faces shining with eager-
    ness . . . gather in a torchlight, midnight tribunal to ride greed,
    lust and murder out of town.
       Skies Blaze Red. . . . 5000 torches light the heavens. . . .
    10,000 glowing faces flame with eagerness.
       SEE—the gigantic mobilization of young courageous manhood.
    FEEL—the fury of the mob.[5]
                                    This Day And Age press copy.

2.   See, youth with desire hot glowing
                      See, maiden with fearless eye.
                      Leading our ranks,
                      Thunder the tanks,
                      Aeroplanes crowd the sky.
                      Bring out the old-time musket,
                      Rouse up the old-time fire! [6]
            Campaign song of Corpo Party, *It Can't Happen Here.*

3. The girls have been on the march for several days. . . . But
    their faces beam . . . That's what they sing today, in joyful scorn
    and from an inner impulse, "For us the sun never sets." As if the
    song itself had brought it fresh strength, the sun has fought its
    way into the clear sky and now shines radiantly.[7]
                       Children's story, written by Baldur Von Shirach,
                                    head of Hitler youth.

The emphasis upon youth, fire, and images of light is common to all three documents. "For the Nazis the sun had a special meaning," writes historian George Mosse. "It was . . . the power of light . . . which links man with the cosmos."[8] DeMille was no Nazi, but in praising "the uncontaminated idealism of American youth" and showing the teenagers trampling all over legal safeguards, he clearly was in way over his head. "Fascism in all countries," writes Mosse, "made a fetish of youthfulness. What a contrast this offered to the elderly politicians haggling in parliaments."[9] Haggling, stalling, while nations faded from past, torchlit glories. So *This Day And Age* idealized the legions of the young for cutting through all the stalling and getting to the heart of the matter.

The story was simple. The teenagers are appalled when gangster Garrett (Charles Bickford) eludes a murder charge through the efforts of his "million-dollar mouthpiece." They nearly lynch him and he confesses to the crime. Even when Hollywood verged on the politically desperate in advocating violent means, its ends were still irrelevant. As always, *This Day And Age* identified American problems with hoodlums and shysters. What was new in the film was the seriousness of the crowd's rage against a lack of control, a void in authority. That the source of public dismay was gangsterism was in keeping with Milton Mayer's observation that "in most of present-day Europe, the bogeyman is a political or religious minority; in this country, he has taken the form of a moral minority—the criminal."[10]

Legality was presented as a barrier to the truth. In his courtroom scene DeMille used a montage of law books, objections being raised, and fingers pointed in order to show how due process was in fact a symptom of social illness; it had become a shield for shysters. Rather than observing all the technicalities of law, the students want direct action, and an eye for an eye. They kidnap Garrett and lead him to a brickyard, where thousands more wait, bearing torches and giving high school cheers. "We haven't got time for any rules of evidence," cries their leader, as the gangster is bound and slowly lowered into a pit full of rats, until he confesses. No matter how DeMille tried to finesse his point ("It was not the intention . . . that high school students should tackle their local racketeers in the same way"),[11] the moral was simple: serious ends merited any means necessary. And the Hitlerite rhetoric of the press copy, obviously shaped to somebody's conception of the film's major selling point, only deepens the importance of *This Day And Age*'s playing to the mob. That DeMille emphasized the power of unleashed thousands was noted by a trade review:

> . . . a sensational and courageous film. Its predominant audience value is that it is loaded with that power which excites emotion hysteria [sic] . . . due to the manner in which DeMille has handled mobs of frenzied youths to obtain spectacle, together with the method he has adopted patriotic music to inspire, there is something sublime about the spectacle.[12]

"Hysteria," "frenzied," "sublime": the review would have served well for a Nuremberg rally. DeMille's endorsement of the power of the mob reflected an intense desire for authority and an impatience with indecision and obstacles—obstacles which got defined as the law. As in the gang films, the law could be identified with the state. It grew out of the kind of feeling which led *Vanity Fair* to call for a dictatorship and *Liberty* to declare that "what we need today is martial law."[13] But the director had overplayed his hand, and local reports were generally hostile. "Infantile plot . . . for many adults with a mental age under fourteen [it] will be rated a great film," said the manager of a Nampa, Idaho, theatre. The manager of the Greenville, Illinois, Lyric Theatre reported a "terrible flop . . . never heard a soul say they liked it," while a manager in Columbia City, Indiana, perceived the film as a lot of "high-class hooey. . . ."[14]

A German film based on the children's story *Emil Und Die Detektive* (UFA, 1931. Director, Gerhart Lamprecht) was a gentler *This Day And Age,* but the relationship between the two is instructive. When a thief steals little Emil's money, the youth organizes his friends to search him out. Hundreds strong, growing ever larger, the children find the criminal and march in back of him, all over the city, until he can stand it no more and capitulates. Siegfried Kracauer thought this "juvenile sleuthing . . . suggests a certain democratization of German everyday life," but behind any mass action creating its own legality scarcely lay a viable democracy. Kracauer's rhetoric seems familiar, in light of the earlier three documents:

Light once for all [sic] defeats darkness in that magnificent sequence in which the thief is eventually cornered. Under a radiant morning sun . . . this Pied Piper in reverse tries in vain to escape the ever increasing crowd of children who pursue and besiege him.[15]

Those crowds and that mystical sun would soon find a hero to shine upon in Germany. DeMille's teenagers would fortunately discover no such demigod in America, although candidates emerged. Hollywood's candidate for the post appeared in *Gabriel Over The White House,* one of the real shockers of the period. *Gabriel* carried the search for authority to the point of a ringing endorsement of an American dictatorship. Like *This Day And Age,* it was typical enough of Hollywood for gangsters to loom disproportionately as the basis of social evil. But its writ ran far wider; *Gabriel,* produced by William Randolph Hearst's Cosmopolitan Studios, was, as Walter Lippmann noted, "a dramatization of Mr. Hearst's editorials." Yet it grew out of a fear which Lippmann himself had voiced the year before: "the danger is not that we shall lose our liberties, but that we shall not be able to act with the necessary speed and comprehensiveness." [16]

Gabriel, in its darkest aspects, anticipated, in praise rather than condemnation, key points of Lewis' *It Can't Happen Here.* In Hearst's vision, it not only could, but should. Made before Roosevelt's inauguration, *Gabriel* caused consternation at MGM, which distributed Cosmopolitan's films. Louis B. Mayer, the studio head and a staunch Republican, thought the film "a slap at recent Republican presidents" and "a piece of propaganda for the incoming administration." [17] But it was Hearst's fantasy, not FDR's. His President Hammond (Walter Huston) obeyed the publisher's deepest instincts: cut through congressional stalling, use national police to eradicate crime, and bully the rest of the world. DeMille's children had found their leader.

At first an old-style reactionary (unemployment and relief are "local problems"), the President sees the light after an automobile accident. Recovering miraculously, he fills the void of authority and becomes a dictatorial presence made in differing parts of Theodore Roosevelt, Abraham Lincoln, and Huey Long. He is granite in feature, solemn in word, aggressive in manner, and unconstitutional in action.

Congress shall, immediately upon our inauguration, initiate amendments to the Constitution providing (a) that the President shall have the authority to institute and execute all necessary moves for the conduct of the government during this critical epoch; (b) that Congress shall serve only in an advisory capacity.   —*It Can't Happen Here* [18]

Lewis' fear was Hearst's dream. His President steps before Congress, declares a state of national emergency, asks the lawmakers to adjourn for the duration of the crisis, and assumes full powers. Deeming Congress "traitorous to the concept of democracy," Hammond urges a dictatorship based "on Jefferson's concept of democracy: the greatest good for the greatest number." He then declares martial law. (Said Bernarr McFadden in June of 1932: "What we need now is martial law; there is not time for civil law. The President should have dictatorial powers.") [19] He sweeps through laws suspending mortgage payments until "average Americans" regain their jobs, and sets up a public works "army" of the jobless.

But *Gabriel*'s dictator, even in Hollywood's most perverse political vision, was not seriously considering any reshaping of institutions outside the federal government. The public works corps will disband as soon as the unemployed "go back into private industry." Instead, hoodlums are again propped up for the ritual slaughter. Hoodlum Nick Diamond directs the assassination of the leader of a jobless march on Washington. Why a mobster is so motivated is never made exactly clear, although it is hinted that he is making money off the Depression. Following the assassination, President Hammond goes after crime. Again, Lewis:

> On a day in late October, suddenly striking in every city and village and backhill hideout, the Corpos ended all crime in America forever. . . . Seventy thousand selected Minute Men, working in combination with town and state police officers, all under the chiefs of the government secret service, arrested every known or faintly suspected criminal in the country. They were tried under court martial procedure; one in every ten was shot immediately.[20]

When Hearst's President gets the government into retail liquor distribution, "muscling in" on the racketeers, gangland seeks retribution against the chief executive. In perhaps Hollywood's moment of supreme madness, the familiar black sedan, which had driven past every doomed sucker who unknowingly strolled down the street or stood behind a glass storefront, rolls up to the White House unimpeded and the hoodlums open fire. President Hammond is unhurt, but the gangsters are through, as well as the Constitution. Writing Lewis' book for him, Gabriel's national police arrest criminal elements en masse. Gangsters are tried by a tribunal composed of the arresting officers and summarily shot by firing squads. What happens to this police apparatus when the criminals are obliterated? Gabriel never says, but Lewis does: They begin shooting the administration's political opponents.[21]

President Hammond ultimately goes after the rest of the world as well. Acting like the Theodore Roosevelt who had answered a younger Hearst's jingoistic prayers, he threatens a war unless world war debts are paid. Lacking funds, the other nations are at his mercy. The film's "hot-headed and violently nationalistic" [22] desires are sated. Hammond dictates a disarmament treaty called, naturally, the Washington Covenant. Predicting future wars in which planes would "bomb cities, kill populations," he signs the Covenant with Lincoln's Emancipation Proclamation quill. As the "Battle Hymn Of The Republic" slips softly into the sound track, the President slumps over and dies, a martyr to peace.

Gabriel's fallen leader is totally credible. What ties Lewis' book to *Gabriel Over The White House*—granting their opposite perspectives—was the Americanization of dictatorship. The novelist's most stunning insight was that American totalitarianism would appear under no foreign guise: it would march in Fourth of July parades and seep out of radios as comfortably as the strains of big bands playing from atop hotel roofs on Saturday nights. *Gabriel*, looking with kindness upon dictatorship, evolved its President out of a tradition as straightfaced and reverent as a grammar school history lesson. Abraham Lincoln stalked the film: his Emancipation Proclamation was a goad to dictatorial action and the "Battle Hymn" closed the film. An American fuhrer would be like the guy next door, and in a time of crisis no one would notice the Bill of Rights being shredded to bits.

Public reaction to film dictatorship was mixed. The manager of a Greenville, Michigan theatre praised it as "one of the best pictures we ever played" and attributed its local failure to the fact that "they don't want the truth nowadays." (Yet apparently a good number of people were drawn to *Gabriel*'s truth; the film was one of April, 1933's top six box office draws.) A Mississippian was expansive: "Well, if I was President of this good old U.S.A., I would okay this great picture . . . it will give them a brighter hope for tomorrow." [23] *The Nation* saw an attempt "to convert American movie audiences to a policy of fascist dictatorship in this country." *The New Republic* bitterly noted that the film "represents pretty well its public." [24]

That public was ready for one more film about presidential authority. In *The President Vanishes*, *Gabriel*'s harshness was avoided and all hints of secret police submerged. What remained was a politician willing to do the drastic, skirt the edges of the Constitution and work his will, but not reshape the government in any important way. The foxy President (fatherly Arthur Byron) has himself kidnapped in order to reroute public opinion and congressional action, which is urging involvement in war.

The fears of 1934 are reflected in the film. A vigilante group called the Gray Shirts, run by a Pelley-esque madman (Edward Ellis) marches for war, beats peace demonstrators and is egged on by munitions manufacturers, revealed to be the brains behind all the war talks. Representing steel, oil, and publishing, they are big time bad guys, forerunners of the right-wing types who would people the later films of Frank Capra.

By setting up marching fanatics and bloodthirsty plutocrats as the foes, *The President Vanishes* makes its chief executive's transgressions seem necessary crisis moves. The Secretary of War (Edward Arnold) assumes effective leadership after the President vanishes and declares, in a radio address, emergency regulations and martial law: "You must be willing to surrender your rights as individuals. . . . Your homes may be invaded." Emergency conditions free the secret service to arrest the munitions clique, killing one who balks at going. The President returns to a chastened public— its fright at his disappearance apparently driving all thoughts of war out of its collective mind. He tells the people (in a radio speech beginning with Roosevelt's "My friends,") that "our struggle is against the forces of selfishness and greed. . . . I don't ask your answer because I know it." As strong as President Hammond, but with more sense of democratic niceties, he intuits the popular will, but it need not be expressed. If its expression is wrong, the President would assume poses drastic enough to change it. The steely *fuhrerprinzip* of *Gabriel* has been made more folksy and a healing liberalism prevails. Instead of establishing secret police, he utilizes the Secretary of War under emergency powers; instead of suspending Congress, he disappears until public hysteria is refocussed; instead of getting world peace at gunpoint, he eliminates the bad capitalists who want war. The ends, to avoid fanaticism and bloodshed, are so unimpeachable that the means seem completely justified. The mob had been mystified and could be manipulated.

The terms of the film indicate what Roosevelt had done to the thrust of *Gabriel* and *This Day And Age*: constitutional uncertainty and benevolent authority had replaced undiluted dictatorship. In late 1934 and 1935, attacks from the right increased in America, yet they represented less a movement into a power vacuum than a fear of creeping socialism. "As the red scare passed away," writes Arthur Schlesinger, Jr., "the fascist dream also waned." [25]

Hollywood's dream was less a fascist fantasy than a longing to

be told what to do, and so starved were some critics for any sign
of political awareness in Hollywood that *Gabriel's* mere mention of
unemployment was seized upon by *The Nation's* William Troy:
"Now for the first time, Hollywood openly accepts the depression
as a fact." [26] The movies always knew that the Depression was
there. What they didn't know, and didn't want to know, was why.

The next time the crowd was portrayed in American film, it
was seen as psychopathic and a "social problem." The two lynching "exposes" of the decade, *Fury* and *They Won't Forget*, saw
social abuse and bigotry at work. Presidential politics was not explicitly involved, yet the films dealt from a position of strength
vis-à-vis the crowd, as DeMille had not. They condemned what
DeMille had figured as a pretty good idea. It is hard not to feel that
this position of strength was tied to a sense that since a leader had
been found, mob action could be safely classified under the heading of "social aberration."

Fury (MGM, 1936. Director, Fritz Lang)
They Won't Forget (Warner, 1937. Director, Mervyn Leroy)
The lynching films developed two themes of the mid-thirties:
distrust of the populace as a whole, tempered by the assumption
of federal benevolence. These themes shaped the tone of *Black
Fury* and *Black Legion* and even more so that of *They Won't Forget*. Leroy concerned himself with the politics and sociology of
lynching, with the act as a social problem which an enlightened
government would have to root out. Like so many Warner efforts
at public education, Leroy's film had the studied concern, depth,
and texture of an editorial cartoon. Fritz Lang, fresh from Germany
and although never the clearest of social analysts (of which his
technically brilliant *Metropolis* gave abundant evidence), was in
no hurry to credit governmental benevolence.[27] He concentrated on
mob irrationality and produced a vastly superior film.

National concern with lynching and mob violence arose because
the number of incidents soared to twenty-eight in 1933, dropped
to fifteen in 1934 and reached twenty-three in 1935. The National
Association for the Advancement of Colored People observed that
some ninety-nine percent of the lynchings committed since 1882

had gone unpunished, and concluded that the problem could no longer be kept in state hands. A federal antilynching bill, drafted by NAACP lawyers, was presented to the Senate in 1934 by Senators Wagner of New York and Costigan of Colorado, and promptly got stalled. In 1935, Southern filibusterers carried the day. The President, loathe to offend Southern committee chairmen, gave the bill no public support.[28]

Roosevelt or not, Leroy seemed sure of his indignation. The setting for *They Won't Forget* was a middle-sized Southern city, ripe with sectional hatreds. When a young secretarial pupil is murdered, a Northern teacher named Hale (Edward Norris) is arrested. An ambitious district attorney (Claude Rains) intends to make his political career by convicting the "Yankee." When the state's fine old Bourbon governor signs a pardon saving the defendant's life, Hale is dragged from a train and lynched. No one is apprehended; the NAACP's analysis was endorsed.

Leroy was praised for depicting a "universal muddiness of soul. . . ."[29] But there was nothing universal about *They Won't Forget*. Leroy was after the South; his small-town DA is a thorough redneck (despite Claude Rains' bungled accent) and the genteel governor the last of a dying breed. The film stayed away from race matters and concentrated on sectional antagonism. One black did appear: a janitor called as a witness was quavering, head-scratching, pitiable. If his qualities were the result of anything in particular, the film kept it implicit. Racial subtleties, however, were not the hallmark of 1937—no film strayed near the subject. Black people bowed or clucked appreciatively at Mr. or Mrs. Whitey. That was it.

Fritz Lang could not so easily sectionalize mob terror and set *Fury* in a kind of Anytown. His populace believes that "in this country, people don't land in jail unless they're guilty" and takes its violence straight. So when Spencer Tracy, a passing stranger, is unjustly jailed on a kidnapping charge, gossip engulfs the town and convicts him without a trial. The town's decent sheriff balks at pressing an indictment, so its citizens storm the jail and burn it down. People smile broadly as the trapped Tracy screams for help; women lift their children to watch the show. The scene is among the most shattering in American film. Where Leroy's governor had unhesitatingly signed the pardon, Lang, with greater political wariness, has his governor up for re-election and loathe to send troops in aid of the besieged sheriff.

If Lang believed, with one of his characters, that sanity was the ability to resist "evil impulses," then he was speaking of an evil in men that seemed to transcend political solution. *Fury*'s small town America revealed a personality which appeared to make federal benevolence somewhat irrelevant. *This Day And Age* felt that mob angers could be ridden to the betterment of the state and boasted in its ad copy, "FEEL—the fury of the mob." A press release for *Fury* was fearful: "They Called it Justice . . . it was the Unreasoning Fury of a Mob." [30]

Lang did not really know what to do with his demonstration of mob violence. Tracy is revealed to be alive, playing dead in order that his tormentors receive death sentences. At their sentencing, however, he relents and walks into the courtroom, declaring that his near-death had destroyed his faith "in justice, civilization . . . feeling that my country was different from all others." Yet he vaguely hopes for a "new life" and embraces his girl (Sylvia Sidney) in the last shot. That a clinch should be the vapid close to this deeply disturbing film indicated Lang's helplessness before the task of converting his demonstration of mob power into a little moral for the audience. For who composed the audience? Some of the very people he had depicted as lynchers. Lang himself admitted his distaste for *Fury*'s ending: "I hated the kiss, because it wasn't necessary. It's such a coy ending now." [31]

Working people, in *Black Fury* and *Black Legion*, had been dealt with severely. *They Won't Forget* took the elitist trend a few steps further: crowd yearnings would have to be manipulated by benevolent leadership. If *This Day And Age* and *Gabriel Over The White House*, born of frustration, spoke from the crowd on up, *They Won't Forget*, like *Black Fury* and *Black Legion*, argued from authoritative benevolence to the irrationality of the governed. The topical films and those centered around authority figures and mob violence were all based on the simplest kind of liberal elitism.

OUR DAILY BREAD. Communitarian farmers build an irrigation ditch to save their drought-plagued farm in the closing section of King Vidor's film. (Courtesy of United Artists Television.)

G–MEN. The FBI agent as screen idol. James Cagney joins up and wins over Margaret Lindsay. (Courtesy of United Artists Television.)

BULLETS OR BALLOTS. Edward G. Robinson likewise goes with the tide: a lawman who pretends to join up with mobsters like Humphrey Bogart. He wrecks Bogart's mob. (Courtesy of United Artists Television.)

WILD BOYS OF THE ROAD. Frankie Darro (in cap) and other hobo youth ask for jobs. (Courtesy of United Artists Television.)

I AM A FUGITIVE FROM A CHAIN GANG. The very nadir of hopes and aspirations as represented on the screen. Star Paul Muni is at extreme left. (Courtesy of United Artists Television.)

BLACK FURY. Coal miner Joe Radek (Paul Muni) and girl friend (Karen Morley) strike a weary pose from this muddled film about labor problems. (Courtesy of United Artists Television.)

THIS DAY AND AGE. Gangster Garrett (Charles Bickford) is nearly lynched by high school crime-fighters, in Cecil B. DeMille's 1933 hymn to mob action. (Courtesy of Universal Pictures.)

Frank Capra. (Copyright 1970, Columbia Pictures Industries, Inc.)

IT HAPPENED ONE NIGHT. Ellen Andrews (Claudette Colbert) and Peter Warne (Clark Gable) in the process of creating screwball comedy. (Copyright 1970, Columbia Pictures Industries, Inc.)

IT HAPPENED ONE NIGHT. The much loved hitch-hiking sequence, a wonderful example of Capra's artful Americana. (Copyright 1970, Columbia Pictures Industries, Inc.)

MR. DEEDS GOES TO TOWN. Longfellow Deeds (Gary Cooper) unites city and country. Babe Bennett (Jean Arthur) loves him. (Copyright 1970, Columbia Pictures Industries, Inc.)

MR. DEEDS GOES TO TOWN. Deeds the democrat is awkward at dealing with servants. (Copyright 1970, Columbia Pictures Industries, Inc.)

MR. DEEDS GOES TO TOWN.
Deeds the distributor of free land
is committed to an institution by
shyster lawyers. (Copyright 1970,
Columbia Pictures Industries, Inc.)

ANGELS WITH DIRTY FACES. The priest as socializing agent. Father
Donnelly (Pat O'Brien) coaxes boyhood pal Rocky Sullivan (James Cagney)
into going sissy before his electrocution to discourage the nation's young
from a life of crime. (Courtesy of United Artists Television.)

DEAD END. Dead End kid Billy Halop is led away to the reformatory as sister Drina (Sylvia Sidney) and the other Dead Enders look on. (Courtesy of United Artists Television.)

DEAD END. Homicidal Babyface Martin (Humphrey Bogart) explains his craft to idealistic architect Dave (Joel McCrea, *left*) and Dead End kid Huntz Hall. (Courtesy of United Artists Television.)

DEAD END. Dead End kids Huntz Hall, Leo Gorcey, and Gabriel Dell direct some class hatred at Ward Bond, doorman at a luxury apartment building. (Courtesy of United Artists Television.)

THE PLOW THAT BROKE THE PLAINS. Okies hiding from the inescapable dust, in this documentary released by the U.S. Government. (Courtesy of Pare Lorentz.)

10

Frank Capra and Screwball Comedy, 1931–1941

Film comedy in the early thirties had blown things apart. Destructive and corrosive, the Marxes and Fields and Lubitsch had been of a piece with the cold-eyed, suspicious and edgy spirit of 1930–1933. In the mid-thirties, something new emerged: a comedy at once warm and healing, yet off-beat and airy. Film historians would label this phenomenon "screwball" comedy.[1] The titles are familiar: *It Happened One Night*, *Mr. Deeds Goes To Town*, *My Man Godfrey*, *You Can't Take It With You*, *Easy Living*, *Nothing Sacred*, and *The Awful Truth* have endured the years with grace and verve. And for good reason. They were (and remain) very funny, perfectly paced, and alive with good humor and terrific people. They left one with what Frank Capra, the most notable of the "screwball" directors, called "a glow of satisfaction."[2]

The glow was genuine: screwball comedies were received with love and are to this day. (One has only to attend a screening of *Mr. Deeds* or *It Happened One Night* to see the hold these films still have over their audience, especially those who remember them from the thirties.) They were special films, for a number of reasons.

First, they brought out the best in a number of incredibly attractive and talented actors and actresses. In Capra's *It Happened One Night,* Clark Gable came into his own as an ironic masculine presence, played off against Claudette Colbert's uncertainty and dewiness. Jean Arthur (*Deeds, You Can't Take It With You, Easy Living,* and *Mr. Smith Goes To Washington*) had the most wonderful speaking voice anyone had ever heard: she was the one movie star men could actually visualize marrying. Carole Lombard quivered with easily cured neuroses in *My Man Godfrey* and *Nothing Sacred* and was a beautiful comedienne. Capra turned Gary Cooper, in *Deeds* and *Meet John Doe,* into the off-beat embodiment of small-town simplicity, honesty and common sense.

But the overwhelming attractiveness of the screwball comedies involved more than the wonderful personnel. It had to do with the effort they made at reconciling the irreconcilable. They created an America of perfect unity: all classes as one, the rural-urban divide breached, love and decency and neighborliness ascendant. It was an American self-portrait that proved a bonanza in the mid-thirties.

Lewis Jacobs has stated the conventional view: "If 'screwball' comedies successfully turned the world on its ear, that was perhaps the way it already looked to a depression generation which felt cheated of its birthright." [3] The "screwball" quality is taken as a kind of veneer, a desperate cover for Depression-bred alienation. Arthur Knight soberly notes that these comedies had "as their points of departure the terrible realities of the period—unemployment, hunger and fear." [4] Neither perspective really seems to work. The screwball comedies were very much a response to the Depression, but not in the tradition of alienation implied by Jacobs and certainly not as the socially aware documents Knight attempts to make of them. Simply stated, the comic technique of these comedies became a means of unifying what had been splintered and divided. Their "whackiness" cemented social classes and broken marriages; personal relations were smoothed and social discontent quieted. If early thirties comedy was explosive, screwball comedy was implosive: it worked to pull things together.

FRANK CAPRA'S AMERICA

Frank Capra's early years could be textbook assignments on the humble beginnings of great men. The Capras arrived in California from Sicily in 1903, and young Frank started hawking newspapers to help keep the poor family solvent. Graduating from high school at a precocious fifteen, he entered the California Institute of Technology and worked his way through school, waiting on tables and running a student laundry. He graduated in 1918, entered the service, and emerged from his hitch into a career crisis. Dropping chemical engineering, Capra drifted, did farm work, was an extra in some westerns, and sold dubious mining stock to gullible farmers and farmers' wives. Going from door to door, he became a "tinhorn gambler and petty financial pirate." [5]

Capra's movie-making vocation began as part of his quest for some easy money. Arriving in San Francisco, he told a local producer, "I'm from Hollywood," and was hired to direct "cine-poems" for seventy-five dollars per week.[6] From that point in the mid-twenties, Capra was set in pictures, blossoming into a major director in the early thirties, and becoming a star director with *Lady For A Day* in 1933. In 1934, Capra got Columbia Pictures to purchase, for five thousand dollars, the rights to a Samuel Hopkins Adams story entitled "Night Bus." MGM lent the services of a second-rank star named Clark Gable, and Capra borrowed Claudette Colbert from Paramount. Neither star was enthused by the prospect of working at Columbia, at that time a decidedly second-class studio. The budget was minimal. Nevertheless, *It Happened One Night* became *the* picture of 1934, stirring a genuinely spontaneous wave of affection throughout the country, playing return engagements and making the fortunes of Columbia, Colbert, Gable, and Frank Capra.[7] Screwball comedy dominated the rest of the decade.

Capra's erratic background was reflected in his best films. The seemingly wide-eyed immigrant boy who travelled the traditional path to success in college (carrying trays in the commons, pen and slide rule concealed beneath the white jacket) was obviously one with faith in the classic American route to opportunity and fulfillment. But the Capra who hustled farmers and sold coupons to their wives, the Capra who turned from chemical engineering to the glib sales pitch and "I'm from Hollywood," was more cold-eyed than wide-eyed. Those two Capras—immigrant dreamer and con man—gave a peculiarly attractive and beguiling quality to his best work. He had a perfect pitch for Americana, for depicting what he passed over as American types, and a sheer genius for manipulating those types. Capra's comedy was a wide-eyed and affectionate hustle—the masterwork of an idealist and door-to-door salesman.

CAPRA'S FILMS, 1934–1941

It Happened One Night (Columbia, 1934)
Mr. Deeds Goes To Town (Columbia, 1936)
Lost Horizon (Columbia, 1937)
You Can't Take It With You (Columbia, 1938)
Mr. Smith Goes To Washington (Columbia, 1939)
Meet John Doe (Warner, 1941)

Before creating the screwball comedy, Capra seemed comfortable with the shyster mania that prevailed between 1931 and 1933. *Platinum Blonde* (Columbia, 1931) showed his initial sympathy with, and attraction to, newspapermen and their racy urban milieu. His hero was an urban Mr. Deeds, an individualist ace reporter with disdain for a world of "phonies." By 1936, the "phonies" would include those very newspapermen. In 1932, Capra directed a movie about bank failures entitled *American Madness*, with Walter Huston the beleaguered and incorruptible banker, kept afloat during the panic by the faith of his depositors.[8] That kind of faith was typical of Capra.

His next vehicle, *Lady For A Day*, was taken from a Damon Runyon story ("Madam La Guimp"), and the choice of material indicated Capra's continued affection for the shyster city. Runyon's world was peopled by the breezy and the sleazy of a Broadway long since gone. Capra revelled in the efforts of various blondes, race touts, and gamblers to pass off "Apple Annie" as a lady of wealth to secure her daughter's marriage to royalty. Eventually, the police and Mayor and Governor of New York pitch in to bring off the deception. It was all urban, this unity—a cheerful combine of all the types Capra would turn against in *Deeds*.[9] A different city— cynical and destructive—appeared in his work from 1934 on.

In the late thirties, Capra evolved the shyster into a vaguely fascistic threat. The urban sharper became the Wall Street giant, communications mogul, munitions kingpin, and reactionary political force embodied in the corpulent and bespectacled figure of Edward Arnold. Capra's emphasis upon the melting of class tensions changed as the decade ended. Class amiability, the end of *It Happened One Night* and *You Can't Take It With You* (and non-Capra works like *My Man Godfrey* and *Easy Living*), became a means. If the mid-thirties witnessed a stress on the resolution of social tensions, Capra, by 1939, fancied that resolution to be an accomplished fact. And so the common decency of all Americans, rich and poor, got turned, in *Mr. Smith* and *Meet John Doe*, against threats to our most sacred national institutions. Capra was exchanging the symbols and dynamics of the thirties for those of the forties.

*   *   *   *   *

With *It Happened One Night*, the first of the screwball comedies, Capra began to turn against the city. His central character, Peter Warne (Gable), was a newspaper reporter and had all the qualities the early thirties had bestowed upon that role: brash, resilient, more interested in sensation than in personal financial gain. He was a man of the city. Yet Capra added dimensions to his character that pointed toward liberation from the iron-clad cynicism of the New York reporter: a vague idealism and dreaminess that aimed at escape, an offbeat cockiness that could effect that escape. Capra's two greatest films—*It Happened One Night* and *Deeds*—both involved the liberation of newspaper reporters. In *Deeds*, the reporter would stand for a whole range of debased urban values, but Gable's role is more complex. He was part hack reporter, part Longfellow Deeds, the small-town idealist.

He hates the newspaper world and vaguely yearns to get out. "I saw an island in the Pacific once," he tells millionairess Ellen Andrews (Colbert). "Never been able to forget it." But he is still the wise-cracking news hawk, feuding with his editor and hot for scoops. And adjusting that great thirties hat (brim down), Gable looked the perfect reporter. When he comes across the heiress Ellen Andrews, she is attempting to escape from her father (Walter Connolly) by bus. She remains at his side, at first out of fear that he will reveal her whereabouts and then, inevitably, out of love. From the process by which mutual cynicism melted before romance evolved screwball comedy.

The "screwball" act was individualistic, idiosyncratic, and, above all, disarmingly open. Capra said that his films insisted upon characters who "are human and do the things human beings do—or would do if they had the courage and the opportunity." [10] His central characters had both. When their night bus is halted by a torrential rain, Warne unhesitatingly takes a single room for himself and the skittish millionairess—and then proceeds to hang a blanket between their beds, calling it the "wall of Jericho." The blanket separates, but the offbeat act of putting it up brings them closer together. They wisecrack over it, get comfortable with each other. The fact that Ellen is short of funds and dependent on Warne's lower middle-class street wit just to survive foreshadows the ultimate melting of class barriers between them.

In a famous hitch-hiking episode, Gable nailed down his stardom when he claimed to have perfected all the nuances of the thumb. He completely fails. Colbert demonstrates her own resourcefulness by stepping to the road, raising her skirt, and bringing the first car to a screeching halt. Both having demonstrated their "screwballness," their class differences disappear. Audiences loved them and loved Capra—for their daring, and his.

When her father's private detectives come pounding on their motel door, the couple inventively phases into a comic, mock married squabble: he the exasperated slob of a husband, she the shrill and hysterical plumber's daughter. The detectives exit in confusion, mumbling about "wrong room"—and Peter and Ellen draw even closer. It set the pattern for all screwball comedy: each act of inventive fancy resulted in greater unity. And in *It Happened One Night*, as in most screwball comedy, that invention broke down walls rooted invariably in class. Peter and Ellen—he a working stiff, she with millions—come to each other with strong initial antagonisms. At the film's beginning, he is full of loathing for her world of wealth and society parties, full of contempt for her flight to marry a playboy named King Westley. Peter calls her a "spoiled rich kid. . . . Haven't you ever heard of humility? You, King Westley, your father are all a lot of hooey to me." She is put off by his brashness, appalled and secretly thrilled by his world.

But Capra, Colbert, and Gable were hardly about to lead us to class warfare. The director discovers rich stores of "screwballness" and good humor not only in the young couple but in Ellen's wealthy father as well. Having made his fortune by tough initiative, not sloth, he greatly prefers Peter's individualistic strength to the idle, polo-playing wealth of Westley. He therefore helps effect his daughter's marriage to Peter. Walking down the aisle on the day of her scheduled wedding to Westley, he turns to Ellen and whispers "You're a sucker to go through with this" and informs her that a car waits. Clad in white, the bride dashes away from the elaborate ceremony, as the assembled guests stand in horror, to the arms of Clark Gable.

The good sense of the wealthy father should perhaps be no surprise; one acute analysis of Hollywood's attitudes toward the rich noted that the "rich household itself is fumed against, but the kingpin of the household is not." [11] The leftist *New Theatre* was appalled at the "wish-fulfillment" involved in the portrait of "a grumpy plutocrat who, of course, had a heart of gold. *It Happened One Night* took place in a social and economic vacuum." [12] It was not so much a vacuum as a fantasy. For Capra, Americans were all the same—social class served as a character, rather than an economic, definition. Beneath the silk hats were common men who had ridden their initiative all the way. "Class" conflicts, in mid-thirties comedy, were really personality conflicts, and hence easily resolved by a good chat. So at the unifying conclusion of Capra's *You Can't Take It With You*, super-plutocrat Edward Arnold whips out his harmonica and plays along with the "whacky" Vanderhof family, immediately embracing their values.

With the wealthy father simply John Doe writ large, carrying a contract-filled briefcase rather than a lunch bucket, Capra helped reinforce an important myth in America. And the myth was rarely as important as in the mid-thirties, when the pieces of the old success formula were being carefully glued back together. Robert and Helen Lynd quote a 1936, Muncie, Indiana, editorial on the subject:

NEARLY ALL ARE IN "WORKING CLASS"

In the United States . . . every man has worked who had the ambition and the opportunity to do so. There has been no class of idle rich. The average industrialist has put in as many hours as the salaried man or wage earner, and he often points with pride to the number of jobs he has been able to afford for others through the effort of his own thrift, intelligence and industry.

. . . The great danger is that an attempt at redistribution of wealth, through increasingly high taxes, will end in poverty and misery for all, as has been the case in Russia. But there is another danger which is just as great—a danger that the United States will become a nation of class-conscious haters. Such a condition will spell the end of American prosperity and progress.[13]

The Alexander Andrews type was by no means limited to Capra. As Barbara Deming observed:

. . . film after film is obedient to a compulsion to clear of any serious censure the big money man, the big breadwinner. . . . Censure of the idle rich but not of the rich who work for their money is of course in the Puritan tradition. And it is in that tradition for a millionaire to be identified with . . . the common man. For is he not just that—the common man who has fulfilled himself? [14]

Other successful screwball comedies picked up on this trend. *My Man Godfrey* (Universal, 1936. Director, Gregory LaCava) set "hobo" William Powell (really a Boston blueblood) as a butler in the bizarre household of the fabulously wealthy Bullock family.

Carole Lombard floats about in a starry stupor, her mother exists in total befuddlement, but the head of the house, Eugene Pallette, is rock solid, a wealthy common man attempting to cope with his "zany" women. Powell finds no trouble in convincing him of a scheme to get the jobless back to work and builds a night club called The Dump on the site of a former shantytown. The hobos get token employment—with vague plans for relief and housing projects come winter.

The *New Theatre* complained of "the familiar condescending paternalism of the upper classes toward their charges—the masses." F. Scott Fitzgerald had seen it even more clearly. "Let me tell you about the very rich," he wrote in 1926. "They are different from you and me. Even when they enter deep into our world or sink below us, they still think they are better than we are." [15] The blue-blood turned "hobo" certainly thought so and Pallette, the wealthy common man, winds up with nothing but *noblesse oblige* toward bums.

Having opened in a hobo camp with Powell, like Henry V, mingling with the masses, *My Man Godfrey* ended with rich and poor together. At The Dump, the rich walk through the doors. The poor hold them open. Thus "the terrible realities of the period" Arthur Knight saw as points of departure. Screwball directors handled depression milieus as if with tongs: their vision depended on it. *My Man Godfrey* placed its faith with the good-natured rich.

So did *Easy Living* (Paramount, 1937). Director Mitchell Leisen presented a soft-hearted Wall Streeter (Edward Arnold) and a plain Jane working girl (Jean Arthur) and left no doubt that some kind of union lay ahead. That Arnold would be delighted to have son Ray Milland marry Jean was preordained. Domestic tranquillity was assured. Maybe Edward Arnold would let your daughter marry his son. Maybe Eugene Pallette would lend you money.

"MR. DEEDS GOES TO TOWN"

In 1936, Frank Capra was surely encouraged to extend his "screwball" perspective. *It Happened One Night* had become one of the great triumphs of American film, both financially and in winning all major Academy Awards for 1934: best film, screenplay, director, actor, and actress, the only film ever to achieve such a sweep.[16] *The Nation* noted the "wholly spontaneous response with which the picture was received." [17]

Confident of his audience, Capra turned to the small-town hero and away from the city. Longfellow Deeds (Gary Cooper) is set against the slick morality, fortune-hunting and cynicism of the shyster city, neutralizes its debasing influences, and emerges ascendant. If he had felt at home with newspapermen and Broadway sharpers between 1931 and 1933, Capra now turned against them and made them stand for the decline of the nation's traditional verities—rooted in village virtues.

Through *Mr. Deeds Goes To Town* parade all the sleek, compromised figures of the early thirties, all those men with the little mustaches: headline-crazy newsmen, society swells, corrupt lawyers, and a jeering public. In a series of encounters with Deeds, their cynicism gets blunted and turned against them.

The plot line bestowed upon Deeds an inheritance of twenty million dollars. He responds, "Twenty million! That's a lot, isn't it?" and turns to play his tuba. A screwball. Brought unwillingly to New York from his little home in Mandrake Falls, Deeds gets housed in a mansion complete with butlers, bodyguards, and a rasping, jaded press agent played by Lionel Stander, the incarnation of Broadway cynicism. Besieged by the city's jackals, Deeds refuses to be taken in and begins showing up New York's corrupted value system.

He withholds his power of attorney from the shysters who seek it. He dismisses fortune-hunters: a lawyer with a competing claim, a society belle named Madame Pomponi (the comic strip name indicating the quality of Capra's urban demonology) and the "opera board." This board requests $100,000 to cover its losses: Deeds, the practical Yankee, rebels. If the opera is losing money, "there must be something wrong." It must give "the wrong kind of show." Profit is the practical, small-town yardstick here, and his screwball individuality in rejecting the request works a unity. Press agent Stander delights in the rebuff to the snobs and starts warming toward his yokel boss.

Deeds wins over the newspaper crowd by melting the tough exterior of reporter Babe Bennett. Assigned to keep Deeds on the front page, she insinuates herself into his guileless affections and relays his exploits (slugging arrogant New York literati, drunkenly feeding doughnuts to a horse), to laughing, heartless New York. But when Babe hears his raptures in front of Grant's Tomb ("I see an Ohio farm boy becoming a great general . . . becoming President"—the first touches of the patriotic sentimentality which would engulf *Mr. Smith Goes To Washington* and which Capra did so brilliantly), she comes to his side, loving the innocence she fears she has lost. And the fact of her small-town origins only solidifies her unity with Mr. Deeds. Soon her editor is likewise protecting him from the urban predators.

Capra shrewdly added some topicality to *Deeds*, and made his hero virtually untouchable, except by those who advocated corruption and starvation. A hungry farmer breaks into Deeds' mansion, waves a pistol about, and breaks down in despairing sobs. Deeds, to the horror of all the shysters, decides to sink his entire twenty million into small farms to be distributed to the needy poor. What was called Capra's *"Saturday Evening Post* socialism" [18] was simply benevolence from above. What made it seem like more was Deeds' small-town, tuba-playing character, his "screwballness." His idiosyncracies were simply small-town virtues disdained by Shyster City. Deeds the village democrat forbids his butler from getting down on his knees; Deeds the village prankster slides down the bannister of his mansion; the fair-minded Deeds realizes he must share his wealth. Importantly, the wealth is a fluke to begin with. Not earned by initiative or wisely invested or saved—just given. There was nothing to do but give it away: the objects of the philanthropy—small farmers and land rather than libraries—made it seem more daring than it really was. Such was Capra's skill that he used this last "screwball" act to unify virtually everybody.

When corrupt lawyers, in a desperate attempt to prevent the hero from distributing his fortune, claim him insane and have him institutionalized, city and country join to vindicate Deeds. Deeds wins over the judge, who calls him, as the poor farmers and newspapermen cheer him on, "the sanest man in the courtroom."

Yokels and city slickers, city and country, rejoice; Deeds and Babe embrace, in love. All is reconciliation. "Goodness, simplicity, disinterestedness," wrote Graham Greene, "these in his hands become fighting qualities." The Broadway crowd, observed Richard Griffith, "end by applauding his rejection of the metropolis and all that it stands for." [19]

Deeds stayed near the top in the box office sales in April and May of 1936. "One of those pictures," said a theatre owner in Eminence, Kentucky, "that people tell their friends about." A theatre manager in Fort Worth was "flabbergasted," and a truly captive audience in Trenton, New Jersey's State Prison told the institution's recreational director "how much they enjoyed it, which is rather unusual, our audience being much more prompt to voice disapproval than approval of films." [20]

Richard Griffith attempted to assess *Deeds'* popularity and concluded that behind Capra the Humanitarian lay Capra the Coupon Salesman:

> The thesis of this sentimental comedy was welcomed by huge sections of the American public. What need for the social reorganization proposed by the New Deal if prosperity and peace could be recovered by redemption of the individual? This idea, absolving the middle-class from realistic thinking about the forces which governed their lives, has proved perennially popular. [21]

But faith in the easy melting of social tension and appreciation of the New Deal were certainly not contradictory impulses. In 1936, Franklin Roosevelt proved at least as popular as Longfellow Deeds. Farm belt and city, middle class and poor voted for the buoyant, endlessly resourceful President. An illusory electoral unity reigned.

Capra would not concern himself with national politics until *Mr. Smith Goes To Washington* and *Meet John Doe*. In *Deeds*, he was concerned with constructing a nearly all-embracing unity by having his village type force the urbanites to accept his values. The film ran the "back to the earth" formula in reverse; rather than advocating return to the land, Capra attempted to bring the values of the country back to the city. Alistair Cooke observed that the director was "starting to make movies about themes instead of people" and Robert Stebbins told New Theatre readers of Capra's "underlying . . . implication, if not recognition, that the world is a place of sorrows, where the great multitude of men suffered for the excesses of a few." [22]

But socially conscious Weltschmerz was scarcely Capra's stock in trade; his optimism was infectious, his contrivance of unity stunning, and his manipulation of the old symbols of shysterism the work of a Hollywood virtuoso. He was steeped in Hollywood's character types. The wide-eyed immigrant boy could effortlessly pull social synthesis out of the America which existed in his imagination; the coupon salesman sensed friendly territory in 1936.

1937–1941

Where could Capra go from the social unity of Deeds? Into the ethos of World War Two. In 1937, he took James Hilton's tale of Shangri-La and filmed Lost Horizon. The social togetherness wrought on Broadway was assumed to exist in the Himalayas. Perfect peace reigned in Shangri-La: inner and outer tranquillity kept men from aging. Because no social conflict existed to begin with, Capra found himself with nothing to work toward. He repeated himself, was talkier than usual and, seen today, Lost Horizon suffers, despite many beautiful touches. Its static quality was inevitable once unity was assured.

Capra returned to more familiar ground in filming the Moss Hart-George S. Kaufman play, You Can't Take It With You, but began changing his villains, once he had disposed of the shysters. The heroes are individualists: a carefree, zany family and its satellites living in a house scheduled to be demolished in the construction of a giant munitions plant. Grandpa Vanderhof (Lionel Barrymore) has not worked in years, but contentedly maintains his stamp collection; his daughter (Spring Byington) writes plays in order to make use of a typewriter; a son-in-law makes fireworks; one granddaughter studies ballet and pirouettes about the house, and the other granddaughter is Jean Arthur. Capra set this crew against the banker and munitions king Kirby (Edward Arnold), linked Jean Arthur romantically with Kirby's son (James Stewart), and laid the groundwork for a final unity. This involved Kirby's seeing the wisdom of Grandpa's crackerbarrel bohemianism and giving up his cartel. Kirby whips out his harmonica and plays along with Grandpa as the film closes, having totally accepted a subversive philosophy of absolute freedom and tolerance for everybody's foibles.

While the unity was an absurdity, Kirby's character indicated the shift in Capra's demonology. While he is surrounded by shyster lawyers, Kirby is no early thirties crook. He seems very much the cold-blooded monopolist, building a munitions empire to capitalize on the day of conflict. As noted in a profile in *The New Yorker*, Capra was very conscious of how he was developing his characters:

Realizing that Messrs. Kaufman and Hart had somehow overlooked the true implications of their major characters, Capra . . . changed Grandpa Vanderhof from a whimsical old madcap to a serious denouncer of those who prefer gold to friends, and the mild and inoffensive Mr. Kirby, who had been a rich boy's father, to a sinister munitions man who causes at least one suicide.[23]

Capra's ending broke him down, but how much longer could the Kirbys of the world be contained?

In *Mr. Smith* and *Meet John Doe*, the comic mode would take second place to Capra's exploration of the evils larger than simple shysterism which seemed to be enveloping the world. Europe's crumbling made simple portrayals of unity impossible. Even Capra couldn't end a movie with Hitler playing the harmonica.

JEFFERSON SMITH AND JOHN DOE

Capra's Jefferson Smith, U.S. Senator, was a variation of the character of Deeds placed in Washington. Played by James Stewart with a genuinely felt conviction, Mr. Smith discovers that the institutions and personalities he revered as the head "Boy Ranger" of his state are rotted from within. After he has been named junior senator of his state, Smith is shocked to see that his state's revered senior senator, Joseph Paine (Claude Rains), is the puppet of Edward Arnold. His power escalating with each film, Arnold now controls the state's newspapers, industries, and politics. Smith decides to buck this near-totalitarian grip, drawing inspiration from the Lincoln Memorial and Capitol Dome (Capra evoking patriotic spirit from these symbols with the clarity and fervor of the successful immigrant, like no one has before or since). Smith learns the consequences: the Arnold-controlled press and radio are turned against him. The one paper that supports his position (the "Boy Ranger" weekly) is seized by Arnold's thugs and, getting even uglier, his supporters are hosed and beaten. Senator Paine erects an elaborate lie to wreck Smith's career, but the young idealist embarks on a filibuster, refusing to stop talking until he, and his nation, have been vindicated.

Why Capra was doing all this, in 1939, suddenly becomes very clear. As Smith held the Senate floor, the director brought in the veteran radio newsman H. V. Kaltenborn to spout breathlessly into a large, round CBS microphone, "democracy in action," and to announce that German and Italian diplomats were in the gallery to see how the process worked. The relationship between the Arnold machine and the politics of these diplomats was far from esoteric.

As Smith held out against everything that was rotten in the world, Capra really began orchestrating the symbols of the 1940s. A simple American like Jefferson Smith, with plenty of idealism and gumption (and the urgings of Jean Arthur, again in the role of cynic turned believer), could fight the complex, shadowy, and undemocratic forces that were darkening the globe. Capra managed the situation like the virtuoso he was: Smith on the Senate floor, sapling-straight and eyes teary; Smith going to the Lincoln Memorial for a chat with the Great Emancipator; fat Edward Arnold screaming orders into telephones. A nation in its movie theatres was being girded for war, by the old master of belief. When Senator Paine admits the truth, Smith is vindicated, but the end was not unity, rather it was a reinforcement of faith in the emblems of democracy.

In *Meet John Doe*, Capra expressed his faith in common Americans ("I have a definite feeling," he told *The New Yorker*, "that the people are right. People's instincts are good, never bad.") [24] in the face of the kind of threat raised in *Mr. Smith Goes To Washington*. Edward Arnold repeats his role, except that by 1941 Capra made even more explicit the kind of danger he was talking about: Arnold, the wealthy publisher, industrialist, and politician, now has a private police force. He sets up "John Doe" clubs all over the country—clubs of average citizens rallied to the "cause" of common decency and neighborliness—to establish his own political base independent of the two parties. He seems to have absolute control over big business and big labor, leaders of both kowtowing to him throughout the film. But the spirit of John Doe (Gary Cooper—a washed-up baseball player picked to be the public symbol of John Doe) was the spirit Capra brought to the approaching war: "We're the people and we're tough. A free people can beat the world at anything . . . if we all pulled the oars in the same direction." Recognizing their common interests (the defeat of antidemocratic evil), Americans could rejoice in their classlessness and vanquish the Nazis.

Cooper had beaten back the "threats" of the early thirties in *Deeds*; now he confronted the steely menace of the forties. Instead of being a stooge, Cooper turns against Arnold at a huge ballpark rally and reveals the plans for political power. He is chased by Arnold's private police force, but his decent voice, like Smith's, like Deeds', could not be stilled. After *Meet John Doe*, Capra would direct the *Why We Fight* series for the United States Government, shoring up the home front. But he had, in fact, begun showing why we would fight with *Mr. Smith*.

To see the Capra films from 1934 to 1941 is to learn more about a nation's image of itself than one has any right to expect. How much did Capra create, and how much did he respond to? His classlessness was an obvious fantasy, but the myth obviously was dear to Americans. He created a tradition in effecting the screwball social peace of *It Happened One Night* and responded to tradition in *Deeds* by neutralizing the shyster world, a world very much Hollywood's creation. Once the thirties had been crossed with the nation's basic institutions intact and relatively unscathed, Capra was free to argue from greater strength; fascism was neither his nor Hollywood's creation.

The way in which Capra manipulated images—city, small town, village hero, profiteer, little man, government, radio—represented genius. He understood enough of what people wanted, after the revelation of the screwball comedies' gigantic success, to help create a consciousness, and to build himself into the system. His fantasy of a social unity entered into the quasi-reality of all mass media. Robert Warshow's remarkable insight that, although Americans rarely experienced gangsterism in their lives, "the experience of the gangster *as an experience of art* is universal to Americans," [25] is extremely relevant to Capra. His America was an experience of art.

That world of Deeds and Smith and Doe had become part of the nation's self-image. No one knew that better than Frank Capra. "I never cease to thrill at an audience seeing a picture," he said. "For two hours you've got 'em. Hitler can't keep 'em that long. You eventually reach more people than Roosevelt does on the radio." [26] By the time he started the *Why We Fight* series, Capra could know that Americans were fighting for, among other things, Frank Capra films.

11

A Solution to Environment: The Juvenile Delinquent

In the late thirties, Hollywood attempted to resolve the environmental questions which the gangster movies had avoided. *The Public Enemy*, for all its stated intentions, had not been prepared, in 1931, to "depict an environment, rather than glorify the criminal." While fearful of making its dynamic protagonist look too good, the film lacked all means to tie together childhood, surroundings and crime. Its "environment"—those turn-of-the-century saloons in which little Tommy Powers dodged through the legs of derby-hatted men—hardly guaranteed criminal behavior. But in 1931, the pressure to explain criminality was low, and gangsters did not have to appear as the end products of some social dislocation.[1] What created them was not shown on screen, it sat in front of the screen: an audience hungry for individual achievement.

Between the making of *The Public Enemy* and *Dead End* (1937), a credible way of explaining gangsters evolved. Hollywood breathed life back into the popular symbols of the law between 1931 and 1937, so criminality could be depicted as something other than a life-style. G-Men and cowboys returned dynamism to the law, the topical films made "concern" cinematic scrip and established federal benevolence as a convention. In the thirties, Hollywood learned how to package social problems and make them dramatically workable.

With the law on a firmer footing, Hollywood found the time ripe, in 1936 and 1937, to "depict the environment"—and discovered the juvenile delinquent. Tough kids with good hearts appeared in *Dead End, Angels With Dirty Faces, Crime School,* and *The Devil Is A Sissy,* among others. The criminal became less a success story than a victim of environmental disadvantage. Not merely in juvenile delinquent stories, but in films which discerned motives for criminal behavior in the indifference of society (*The Great O'Malley, You Only Live Once*), the idea of the criminal as victim of his surroundings gained currency. Hollywood's interpretation of environmentalism followed America's discovery of a social agenda: minimum wage, unemployment insurance, social security. Into that quantifiable horizon loomed "better housing." Slums bred delinquents, and that meant the nation had to get its kids off the streets.

KIDS AND STREETS

Dead End and *Angels With Dirty Faces* began to use the gangster city in a new way. The side streets which had stood unobtrusively as gun-laden sedans roared past, the alleys which had existed solely for escape, became protagonists. They filled with people and became The Neighborhood. Streets in gangster movies were invariably empty because gangsters inhabited a city almost entirely their own, a city which, as Robert Warshow observed, became symbolic.[2] But in films about juvenile delinquents the streets provided the context for depicting hoodlums as products of poor social engineering.

The steets were a little stagey. Cameras lingered on children at play (girls sticking their tongues out at boys in caps, boys thumbing their noses at policemen and grocers) and fairly begged for authenticity. In reality, Hollywood was only shuffling its myths. The shyster city was replaced by the city of The Neighborhood, an imagined microcosm of all overpopulated urban areas. In its streets, by its storefronts and tenement stoops, the underprivileged jostled and young boys got into trouble. The Neighborhood was a cheery conglomerate of nationalities: the Jewish tailor waves a needle at the Irish cop, who takes an apple from an obliging Italian grocer and greets a Polish mother. Since the poor had no servants, blacks were nowhere to be found.

The setting *was* the environment, so the camera stayed mostly outside; interior shots were utilized only, as in *Dead End*, to reveal the squalor within. And that squalor produced troubled kids. Hollywood's sociology was cut and dried: even in *Dead End*, boldest of them all, the slums, like the earlier gangsters, appeared ready-made and fully formed. Cause and effect was being taken one step at a time. That gangsters were now being "explained" appeared to be enough; what had brought the slums into being was out of range. The environmentalism of the delinquency films, however, was in no way out of the main currents of social thought in the late thirties. Sadly enough, it was closely in step.

A Note on Thirties Environmentalism

As early as 1853, a report on *Sanitary Conditions of the Laboring Classes In New York* had concluded that the "connection of juvenile depravity . . . with the wretched conditions of [slum] life was obvious." Historian Roy Lubove traced environmentalism over a hundred-year span and noted that simplistic assumptions about cause and effect prevailed throughout. In the 1880s, "housing reformers placed excessive faith in the potency of a changed physical environment." Twenty years later, slum expert Lawrence Veiller "accepted with no reflections the hypothesis that better housing implied not only healthier but morally superior citizens." As late as 1952, a report prepared for the Philadelphia Housing Authority observed that the "policy maker . . . often assumes that it is the *bad housing* in slums which breeds these social disadvantages. . . .

But actually there is not much evidence to show that these poor social conditions were caused by the poor housing *in and of itself*." [3]

The conventional wisdom of the late thirties did not stray far from this formula. A 1936 study entitled *Social Determinants In Juvenile Delinquency* insisted that "if children had opportunities . . . of using their pent-up energies in playgrounds and in other wholesome ways, they would not insist on committing acts that jeopardize the public." [4] (Pat O'Brien would operate on the same principle in *Angels With Dirty Faces*, placing basketballs into the hands of Leo Gorcey, Huntz Hall, and the rest of the Dead End kids. It was the old Police Athletic League mystique.)

How value-laden theories on delinquency were was demonstrated by William Healy's *New Light On Delinquency And Its Treatment*, published in 1936 under the auspices of Yale University's Institute for Human Relations. Healy categorized 133 delinquent families under headings like "both parents dull or subnormal mentally," "superior personality qualities," "father's interests (aside from alcoholism) poor or vicious," "high ethical standards," "poor ethical standards." [5] *The Literary Digest* summed up the thought on delinquency with a fair degree of accuracy:

Sociologists agree that most delinquents are not naturally bad. They are forced through environment, or emotional upsets, into situations where they become delinquents. Boys in clubs or gangs merely are letting off excess energy. They devote the same enthusiasm to the high ideals of the Boy Scouts once they're led to see it's not sissy to be good. Giving them ample recreational activities . . . goes a long way towards keeping them on the straight and narrow.[6]

Concern for the urban environment led to increased demands for new housing under federal subsidies, although government grants to bulldoze the slums were not part of the New Deal: Roosevelt balked despite the urgings of New York's Senator Wagner, who tried in vain to push housing bills through the Senate in 1935 and 1936. A Chicago urbanologist complained that "there may be a new day dawning on the darkness of the housing problem, but there is very little light visible as yet." Finally, in 1937, Congress allocated half a billion dollars (Wagner had asked for a billion) in federal loans to be made available for slum clearance. And the Senator from New York was Samuel Goldwyn's honored guest at the premiere of *Dead End* in August of 1937.[7]

Dead End (United Artists, 1937. Director, William Wyler)
Angels With Dirty Faces (Warner, 1938. Director, Michael Curtiz)
The Devil Is A Sissy (MGM, 1936. Director, W. S. Van Dyke)
Crime School (Warner, 1938. Director, Lewis Seiler)
The Mayor Of Hell (Warner, 1933. Director, Archie Mayo)

Dead End stands as a beautiful document of a nearly vanished consciousness in America. The realism of its tenements was self-conscious, but the concern in the film with social issues was genuine. The film's opening shots—a panoramic sweep of New York City gradually focussing on the river front slum and its neighboring high rental buildings—were visually striking and to the point. As the camera moved to a close shot of the slum, the realism aimed at by the theatre of Elmer Rice and Clifford Odets came briefly alive on screen: we have common people on an average day. The celebration in the thirties of the common man's tribulations, made dramatic by economic deprivation and made stagey by social consciousness, was preserved, in part, in *Dead End*.

Sidney Kingsley's play, *Dead End*, had been performed on Broadway some seven hundred times;[8] when Samuel Goldwyn produced it, the aura of "important play" remained. Authenticity of setting was emphasized, and gave away the film's environmental assumptions. United Artists publicists insisted that *Dead End*'s magnificent set was a duplication of an East River slum, with an eye for detail extending to the inclusion of freshly cut fruit peelings in the water.[9]

It was not the Depression's first film about delinquency, but the looming role of streets and houses clearly set it apart. *The Mayor Of Hell*, released in 1933, dealt with wayward youth, but only to provide an exposé of reform school maladministration and brutality in the style of *I Am A Fugitive* . . . , after which it was modeled. While Warner press agents declared that "no concerted effort has been made to eliminate the environment which leads to petty thievery, hoodlumism and the Reformatory," the film, like *The Public Enemy*, found it impossible to make the links between "conditions" and crime. The press copy was hence equivocal: " 'The Mayor of Hell' Makes Us Wonder How Much of What It Shows Parents Are Responsible For." [10] The tensions that operated in 1933 differed greatly from those of 1937. The delinquents riot under oppressive conditions and murder the reformatory chieftain, who, embracing two early thirties conventions, is both sadist and shyster. As in *This Day And Age*, ends justify the means. But at the film's end, the reform school is upgraded by benevolent jailers and becomes a place to feel at home in, like the chain gang of *Hell's Highway*.

In 1936, MGM's half-hearted *The Devil Is A Sissy* moved partially towards the environmental preoccupation of *Dead End*. Its urban neighborhood spawned bullies such as Mickey Rooney and Jackie Cooper. But when Freddie Bartholemew's father declared "The next generation is finding itself out there . . . on the street," he missed the environmental point that the next generation was losing itself in that very place. *The Devil Is A Sissy* had no idea of what to make of the streets, and its potential delinquents, Cooper and Rooney, were better suited to small-town pranks—ducking away from the school road to go fishing, attaching a funny horn to the old jalopy—than to slum jungles. Louis B. Mayer's heart was ever with Andy Hardy, and Freddie Bartholemew wraps up *The Devil Is A Sissy* by teaching his new-found friends, Jackie and Mickey, to be obedient to probation officers.

But *Dead End*'s kids—Leo Gorcey, Huntz Hall, Billy Halop, Bobby Jordan and Gabriel Dell (all of whom had been in the original Broadway cast)—were absolutely credible. They fight among themselves, dive into the filthy water of the East River, and emulate the toughest hoods of their day. Their parents are drunkards or absentees and their homes are filled with rodents, crying infants, and brawling couples. Their accents were true New York Corrosive, and their facial expressions reflected a mingled sullenness and diminishing hope which was perfect and tragic. The film used these children in two ways: to make the point that decaying houses bred crime, and to bury the gangster myth by reducing that early thirties hero to a sociological cipher.

"The abnormal habits and traits of a transitional society," declaimed a high-sounding press release, "are soon reflected in antisocial behavior of both children and adults alike." [11] The film, thankfully, was less fancy. It opened with a class animosity which the film industry had spent the decade laughing out of existence. Some opening vignettes went this way: A policeman jostles a sleeping tramp. Gritty water splashes against some creaky wooden pilings, around which sit the Dead End gang, dressed very shabbily. The doorman of the adjoining luxury building, whose service entrance symbolically faces (and shames) the slum, barks at the Dead End kids, who deride him in return. Caricatured haughty inhabitants of the luxury building leave by the back and view the tenement dwellers like smears on a slide.

Following this, union-conscious Drina (Sylvia Sidney), sister of Dead Ender Billy Halop, says that she will strike for the money "to get you off these streets," and the Dead End gang beats up an insufferable Fauntleroy who lives in the terraced building. There had been nothing like Dead End's high-voltage class tension in any Depression film.

Through "environment," Dead End found a way to destroy the gangster myth. Tensions of class quite overpowered those of criminality. When the notorious Babyface Martin (Humphrey Bogart)—a spectre from an earlier Dead End gang—returns to the old neighborhood, he is in flight after committing eight murders. Like The Petrified Forest's Duke Mantee (Bogart's brilliant 1936 performance as the gangster isolated in the West, stripped of a success drive by his own neurosis and a renascent law), Babyface is on the fade. Unlike the Duke, he is a strictly urban hoodlum, a gangster whose gang no longer exists. Taken from the context of the gang (and left only with a nervously loyal sidekick, Allen Jenkins), Babyface is terribly exposed. Dead End saw him as the archetypal slum product, the end result of noisome dwellings. Attempting to justify himself to Dead End's hero, Dave the architect (Joel McCrea), Babyface sounds hollow as he runs through the traditional mobster's litany of rewards: "See this shirt? Silk, twenty bucks. See this suit? Custom tailored, a hundred and fifty bucks."

His mother rejects him, his old girl friend has turned to prosti-tution. With no roots but a slum, with confusion replacing am-bition (Dave: "Ever get scared?" Babyface: "Nah. Can't live for-ever . . . I don't know." Rico's answer would have been a dis-believing "Me, yeller?"), he is the early thirties hero now explained as a man whose background has prepared him for the scrap heap. We are no longer shown the process of achievement, only bitter and lonely decline. Bogart's nearly psychopathic brooding was per-fectly suited to the task of de-fusing the gangster myth. He in-dulgently watches the Dead End kids fighting, wistfully recalling his pre-homicidal youth, but ultimately he must confront the future, a future in which social engineering would automate crime out of existence. In *Dead End*, the future belongs, with a sym-bolism which would be ponderous if it were not now so touching, to an architect.

Between Dave the architect and Drina the striker lay Sidney Kingsley's decent, slumless social order. It is Dave who states *Dead End*'s theme: "What chance do they have with all this. Enemies of society, they say. I want to tear these buildings down." It is Dave who mistrusts the rich and goes to concerts in the park. (And thirty-five years later, it is hard not to free-associate from there: lectures on Spain at Town Hall, Russian films, sitting in the balcony for *We, The People*, arguments in luncheonettes near City College—the only time any vague sense of that world ever made its way into a Hollywood film.) [12] Dave is the class-conscious social engineer. Since it is he who will re-shape the en-vironment, it is he who must kill off Babyface Martin, who has been utterly shaped by that environment. But who replaces the gangster, who was, after all, the classic individualist? A social planner who is equally individualistic, or is social planning itself the hero? There is no reason to expect a moving picture to supply answers no one else had, but the questions raised by *Dead End* are helpful in assessing part of the heritage of the thirties. So one is not baiting a film made over thirty years ago by mulling over its central equation: clear the slums and the good life will open wide.

A DIGRESSION: THE GOOD LIFE

Drina raises a profound dilemma which she speaks of striking for the money to get her brother off the streets. What will he leave the streets for? Dave's new housing? The houses themselves appear the end: streets empty, high rises gleaming in the background.[13] It is interesting that, following the success of *Dead End*, the Dead End kids starred in many comedies, with a street vitality which lingered long after Dave and Drina had marched off to reshape the society. What thirties environmentalism failed to come to grips with was the vitality which existed in the streets, and the larger problems to which delinquency was connected. An empty cause and effect—slums, therefore delinquents—remained. A prescient sociologist named Clifford Shaw had sensed the larger issues as early as 1929:

It has been quite common in discussions of delinquency to attribute causal significance to such conditions as poor housing, overcrowding, low living standards, low educational standards, and so on. But these conditions themselves probably reflect a type of community life. By treating them one treats only symptoms of more basic processes. Even the disorganized family and the delinquent gang . . . probably reflect the community situations. In short, with the process of growth . . . the invasion of the residential communities by business and industry causes a disintegration of the community as a unit of social control.[14]

A social order with no sense of human proportions turned the neighborhoods sour. Not merely the physical community disintegrated, but that sense of community which allows people to feel both responsible and responsive to others and consequential in themselves was shattered by ever-increasing political and economic concentration. Thirty years would elapse before one could see that Drina's brave unionism had been legitimized into a countervailing force, a force as powerful, impersonal and unresponsive as those it was designed to neutralize. It is all too fitting that Drina should want union power to get her brother off the streets, and that Dave should dream of slums turned super-city. The sons and daughters of Dave and Drina (and of the Dead End gang) would wonder, years later, exactly why they had been taken from those streets, and would question what their parents had offered as substitutes: a life built around security, a society so rationalized and impenetrable that goals within no longer seemed to exist, a society which created a "good life" without democratic controls over who and what defined that "good life."

Thirties environmentalism became, along with the assumption of federal benevolence, the basis for social action in the post-war period, its relevance rapidly diminishing. What were patent necessities—minimum wages, social security, medical and unemployment insurance, aid to education and housing—became the ends of the society, rather than prerequisites. The sixties would pay dearly for this misjudgment. Labor unions retired from innovation, once the above necessities and their own legitimacy had been gained, and stood aghast as the middle-class young, for whom "conditions" had been perfect, began talking the political radicalism the unions had so quickly abdicated. If *Dead End* had told us that better housing would get children off the streets, what could have brought children out of those split-levels and luxury apartments back into the streets in the 1960s? How could they have forsaken that ideal environment, or question that success model?

Within sociology, a reaction began against environmentalism. By 1954, Bernard Lander, in *Towards An Understanding of Juvenile Delinquency*, opted for an "anomie" theory of delinquency, rather than one based on economic determinism. Pressures other than poverty could disaffect the young [15] and afflict them with a sense of inconsequentiality.

A notion like alienation was distant indeed from the delinquency films of the late thirties—their social problems were made of concrete. But Lander's anomie theory fit 1953–54 well, and the culture responded with Marlon Brando's sullen motorcyclist of *The Wild One*, roaring into terrified hamlets out of sheer boredom, and James Dean's lost high-schooler of *Rebel Without A Cause*, the spawn of an empty and rootless family life. Modes of crime, as always, became metaphorical for tensions in the society, and the delinquents served the mid-fifties as well as the gangsters had served the early thirties. The latter's grim triumphs suited 1930's anxieties about, and longings for the possibilities of individual success; the delinquent reflected the first tensions of a boredom and aimlessness which kept the youth of the fifties quiet and, tuned to a higher pitch, turned the youth of the sixties to drugs and disaffection from the major institutions and values of their society.

But *Dead End* was made in 1937, not 1967. Labor struggle was still bitter and when Drina tells a policeman who chastizes the slum-dwellers for being "cop-haters," "We're strikers; one of you lousy cops hit a striker," it becomes clear that battles were still to be won, that between Drina and George Meany lay a considerable distance. Two months before *Dead End*'s premiere, no fewer than ten persons were killed when striking Republic Steel workers marched on their plant. Drina's anger and class consciousness were not Hollywood fantasies, not in 1937.

Uncertainties remained in *Dead End*. The conclusion was one. "Folks said the ending of this film left you up in the air," said the manager of the Rainbow Theatre in Newport, Washington.[16] It did. Having killed Babyface Martin and seen Drina's brother sent off to reform school, Dave vows to use his reward money to help Drina get a lawyer. The two march off, against great odds, to change their society. Neither has gained any power in the course of the film; how Dave will be able to tear those buildings down is a point Kingsley had left moot enough to rouse the *Daily Worker* into hailing the Broadway production's "sound revolutionary implications." [17]

Such implications never quite made their way into the movie. But gone too was the Warner device of the federal government as *deus ex machina*, miraculously appearing to banish the slums. The best hopes were vague ones—a future of good people like Dave working for the people. *Dead End* created tensions of class which couldn't possibly be resolved within the Warner formula; it would have been incomprehensible, given the bitterness set up between the slum dwellers and their society. Local law is still downgraded:

Drina's brother is mindlessly swept up into reform school, and
the cop on the beat is aware that the locals are "cop-haters."

Given all the class tension and the dismal image of local law
enforcement, who could socialize the delinquents? The social
worker was a Warner answer. Humphrey Bogart played the part
in *Crime School*, but the effort was lackluster. The film was a
re-make of *The Mayor Of Hell*, with the addition of the social
worker character and some chic environmentalism ("if you want
to help these boys, clean up the slums"), but without the riot and
murder. At its conclusion, the Dead End boys were vaguely labelled "good citizens." The problem was how to relate wayward
boys to the society which created them; how to give them options
besides criminality while admitting social inequality. Too honest
to melt class tensions in the mode of the screwball comedies, the
delinquency films nonetheless found it necessary to go beyond
class and find a figure who was classless, within the system, sympathetic to the boys, and dramatically feasible. Always resourceful,
Hollywood called upon the priesthood.

The figure of the priest proved immensely useful to moviemakers. Appearing in short order were Spencer Tracy as Father
Flanagan in *Boys Town*, William Gargan as Father Dolan in *You
Only Live Once*, and Pat O'Brien's Father Jerry Connelly, the
boyhood pal of Jimmy Cagney in *Angels With Dirty Faces*. The
last-named was most intriguing, if only for the presence of the
Dead End kids living in a neighborhood without Dave or Drina.
Her unionism is absent, as is his vague architectural vision and
class-consciousness. Instead, a fairly crude distillation of social
thought remains: the recreational, Police Athletic League ethos.
Angels With Dirty Faces had its priest roll up his sleeves and get
the Dead End kids out on the gym floor, where their anti-social
energies would be good-naturedly expended, and insisted that he
help do away with the gangster. When Jimmy Cagney, like
Bogart, returns to the neighborhood, he runs into his childhood
pal turned priest, the tough turned straight. Just out of prison,
Cagney is asked to help turn the Dead End gang away from a
life of crime.

The boys idolize Cagney (thirty years later, it is still hard not to) and O'Brien uses the hoodlum's vitality to socialize them, goad them into playing basketball. The priest goes on an anti-crime crusade, discovers that Cagney is still deeply involved in the rackets, and turns him in to the law. O'Brien asks Cagney to make an hysterical spectacle of himself en route to the electric chair, in order to turn the kids off forever. Cagney's reply—"You're asking me to give up the only thing I have left"—demonstrated a fine awareness of the doom of the gangster hero; no longer a success story, no longer noble in death. But Cagney complies, and the Dead Enders, at picture's end, are deeply depressed. What do they turn to?

The implications of the delinquency films were all negative: stay off the streets, stay out of trouble, and don't emulate gangsters, who are sapped of their heroic strength. Whose lifestyle was there to copy: that of the priest or the social worker? There is a sad and revealing moment in *Dead End* which speaks to all the uncertainties of the delinquency cycle.

The moment comes about when Drina reveals a fantasy she had: a rich man arrives at her home and takes her away from the slums forever. It is a fantasy right out of the screwball comedies and seems to melt her role as a unionist. Here the failure of the delinquency films is suddenly connected to so much of what went on in thirties films, to why they seemed to hesitate at the brink. It sprang from the dream of the windfall. After all the realism, loving attention to detailed setting, and indignation at injustice, lay the hope that social problems could be wished away, the faith that the Depression would lift and the old competitive energies would be loosed in the land. So Pat O'Brien, with his basketball games and crime crusades, was marking time with the delinquents until the rich man came along and social tensions evaporated. The role of the priest was to keep class anxieties muted —God would enable the Dead Enders to go straight within the slums. But the sense of a culture biding its time is pervasive: aware of social strain, full of benevolence, short of a desire to get to causal roots. Sadly enough for America, the "rich man" came along who wished social tensions away and made even "environment" secondary: World War Two. Division and class strife were to be put aside for the duration: classless G.I.-Joe was ascendant. It is not surprising that the person chosen to inform us "Why We Fight" would be no Kingsley, but rather Hollywood's master synthesizer, Frank Capra.

HUMAN ENVIRONMENT AND CRIMINALITY

The Great O'Malley (Warner, 1937. Director, William Dieterle)
You Only Live Once (United Artists, 1937. Director, Fritz Lang)
   If the delinquency films relied upon physical environment to make their points about nascent criminality, other films attacked the process of going beyond the law from another perspective: the cruelty of the human environment. This was less a matter of class than of institutional indifference. In *The Great O'Malley*, the focus was on the stupidity and blind adherence to regulations of a cop on the beat; in Lang's film, as in *Fury*, on a more compelling fear of widespread lack of compassion, of a cancer in human relations. The difference between the two films was similar to that between *They Won't Forget* and *Fury*: the Warner instinct for social cartoons contrasted to Lang's more basic concern with retribution.

   The Great O'Malley and *You Only Live Once* shared a common characteristic: a concern with personal evil and error. If the delinquency films seemed to substitute "environment" for the bad guys of the early thirties, films about the human environment brought the two traditions together. O'Malley (Pat O'Brien) is a foolish policeman who maintains an absolutist position on all matters of city ordinance. He fines an Italian junkman for having more than three bells on his wagon, busts a tailor for having his awning too near the sidewalk. The bane of his precinct, O'Malley declares "there's nothing more beautiful than a badge." Dieterle turns the film into a sermon on sticking to the rules, while ignoring "conditions" which turn law into hardship. But the law seems independent of the society, rather than its creation and its tool.

   This creates some large confusions. O'Malley prevents a desperate man (again, Bogart) from getting to his first job in years by fining him for a noisy muffler. Bogart, failing to get the job, must turn to crime in order to feed his wife and lame daughter, and is nabbed by the omnipresent O'Malley. While newspapers declaim, "How many men have been driven to crime by this petty persecution," O'Malley's captain tells him, "we want men on the force who can do a little more than their duty." O'Malley has a change of heart, triggered by the sight of Bogart's crippled daughter, but the change seems irrelevant to any social concern. Circular reasoning resulted: society would be the better if policemen recognized that people were being manhandled by their society. Unemployed men should not be bothered about their mufflers—the limits of benevolence were never clearer.

Lang's *You Only Live Once* is really a coda to the environmental theme, although made at the beginning of the cycle. One of the great films of the thirties, *You Only Live Once*, was plainly obsessed by the meanness of spirit and indifference to suffering Lang saw all around him, and concerned with what he saw as common to all his work: "the fight against destiny, against fate." [18]

Lang depicted the gangster as victim—the three-time loser (Henry Fonda) as social outrider. Released from prison, befriended only by faithful Father Dolan (William Gargan) and his girl friend (Sylvia Sidney), Fonda encounters a world which can define him only as a criminal and hence forces him to play out that role. Driven from his honeymoon motel by a shrewish proprietress who comes across his photograph in a "true detective" magazine, fired from a truck driving job for one lateness ("hear that, jailbird"), and assumed to be the culprit in a crime he didn't commit, Fonda is completely boxed in, as was Muni in *I Am A Fugitive* . . . Yet this time the causes are visible: mistrust and an environment which forces recidivism. While *You Only Live Once* was perhaps the bleakest Hollywood product since *I Am A Fugitive* . . . , its world was far different. Lang projected an outrage that outweighed despair—he knew his enemies. *I Am A Fugitive* . . . had been afraid to guess about the system which ruined its hero.

Lang's particularly bleak view of human nature extended a theme of the late thirties, but did not go beyond it. The priest is again the one to relate crime to environment, and when law officers discover (too late) that Fonda has been falsely convicted, they are *federal* agents. But priests and federal lawmen were not enough to redeem Lang's America. Fonda, trapped into a death sentence, escapes from jail and, with his pregnant wife, takes off cross-country. Committing some petty crime, they are branded major brigands. (The similarities to and contrasts with the *Bonnie And Clyde* story are many.) [19]

The two are heartbreakingly done in as we see them move through the cross-hairs of a sheriff's rifle, see them shot, see them fall. As they appear in the rifle sight, they suggest, at once, hunted animals, microscopic beings and wooden figures in a shooting gallery. The image is of sheer control, of an entrapment that reaches beyond environmental message into the realm of tragedy.

The social message declared by one of the characters—"you can't keep a man in the death house and expect him to straighten out his mind just like that"—was the standard compassion of the late thirties. In the Warner formula, Fonda would have been brought back alive, united with his priest, and agreeable to a token five-year stretch, with employment guaranteed upon release. But, as in *Fury*, Lang's dismal assumptions about human nature reign supreme. Despite federal agents discovering the truth about the case, the director left little hope that his problem fell within the realm of governmental solution or institutional change. It lay with changes of the spirit. *You Only Live Once* not only condemns the unfeeling caricatures on screen, but seems to condemn its audience as well. For as Fonda and Sidney appear on the sheriff's rifle sight, we see them as he does and kill them just as certainly. Form and content correspond exactly: the sheriff pulls his trigger with our silent assent. He is society's agent and society has defined Fonda and Sidney as enemies.

The death of early thirties gangsters, whether done in by their own or by the law, made perfect sense. When Cagney is dropped into his mother's living room, swathed in bandages, or a dying Edward G. Robinson gasps, "Is this the end of Rico," we are merely witnesses. Lang forced us to peer through the blank sight of the law, to participate in the killings and the guilt. Social indifference was our indifference. Where Lang's perspective left us was not perfectly clear. After one accepted personal responsibility for society's indifference to suffering, there wasn't much to say or do. Personal guilt for criminal behavior was a profitless field for speculation.

A FINAL ENVIRONMENTAL NOTE: "THE RIVER" AND "THE PLOW THAT BROKE THE PLAINS"

In 1936 and 1937, the United States Government financed the production of two unusual short documentaries: *The Plow That Broke The Plains* and *The River*. Directed by Pare Lorentz, the films fused federal benevolence with the concept of environmental manipulation to engineer the good society. *The Plow* concerned the dust bowl and soil erosion; *The River* focussed on river power and the Tennessee Valley Authority.

Lorentz, "a strong New Dealer," made sure that his patrons would not be offended by the films on land and public power. When two rebellious cameramen, Paul Strand and Leo Hurwitz, balked at Lorentz's quasi-epic conceptualization of *The Plow* and submitted their own script, the director "didn't like it. He said they wanted it to be all about human greed and how lousy the social system was. And he couldn't see what this had to do with dust storms." [20]

The social system was ignored, and we are left with films focussed exclusively and self-consciously on environment. Both films were like WPA murals—all cattle and horses and land, all rolling rivers and timber. The narration stressed a corporate, national "we," as if it were the Nation (and History) talking to itself. "Two hundred miles from water, two hundred miles from town, but the land is new," rumbled *The Plow That Broke The Plains*. From *The River:* "We built a hundred cities and a thousand towns, but at what a cost." It was that kind of narration. While the photography was often brilliant—there are shots of tenant farmers in *The River* that nearly match the photography of Walker Evans—it was somehow cold and self-serving, too concerned with becoming instant myth, too wrapped up with its role in an historical saga of the thirties. The same could be said for Virgil Thomson's folk-tune-filled musical score. When *The River* became obsessed with repeating place names (as if placing sign-posts on history)—"The Yazoo, the Monongahela"—its self-con-sciousness as a Document became very apparent.

Very few people were shown on screen. The role of the citizen was that of the beneficiary of federal help. Except as victim—staring at mounds of dust nearly up to his windows, staring at floods—he had nothing to contribute to this saga. The reclaiming of the land and the re-channeling of river waters for public power were unimpeachable ends. But the nagging question remains: had the travail of the thirties produced no more compelling a vision than that of environmental manipulation to serve a passive, stricken citizenry? "Blown out, blasted out," said *The Plow* of drought-wracked farmers, "nothing to stay for, nothing to hope for . . . All they ask is a chance to start over, to have medical care." But how to start over? In the same competitive market that destroyed them in the first place?

12

Conclusions

No medium has contributed more greatly than the film to the maintenance of the national morale during a period featured by revolution, riot and political turmoil in other countries. It has been the mission of the screen, without ignoring the serious social problems of the day, to reflect aspiration, optimism, and kindly humor in its entertainment.
—Will Hays, 1934 [1]

We were against revolution. Therefore, we waged war against those conditions which make revolutions—against those resentments and inequalities which bred them. In America in 1933 the people did not attempt to remedy wrongs by overthrowing their institutions. Americans were made to realize that wrongs could and would be set right within their institutions.   —Franklin Roosevelt, 1936 [2]

The movies made a central contribution toward educating Americans in the fact that wrongs could be set right within their existing institutions. They did so not by haunting the screen with bogeyman Reds but, as Hays noted, by reflecting aspiration and achievement. They showed that individual initiative still bred success, that the federal government was a benevolent watchman, that we were a classless, melting pot nation.

From 1930 to 1933, it is fairly easy to trace the subject matter and preoccupations of American film and chalk it all up to depression, despair, and anomie. Gangsters, prostitutes, con men, sleazy back-room politicos, lawless lawyers: a dreary parade of characters peopled the movies, bred by a cynical, burnt-out culture. And there *is* that side to it: filmgoers were undeniably attracted to outlaws, observed a paralyzed law slumbering and bumbling, saw a dynamism in dishonest lawyers, and rejoiced at the Marx Brothers war against sanity. But there is another side of this attraction to the lawless and freakish. (Literally freakish. Tod Browning's 1932 MGM film, *Freaks*, had a cast made up of pin-heads, human torsos, midgets, and dwarfs, like nothing ever in the movies. And what more stunted a year than 1932 for such a film.)

And that other side seems more compelling and helpful for an understanding of how the decade progressed. In the gang films and musicals, Hollywood coaxed an old success model back to life, creating special worlds in which it could function. The gangster world and the backstage world of Warner's big three musicals of 1933 were, in effect, success preserves. From triggerman to Boss of the North Side, from back row of the chorus to the opening night lead, from office boy to chairman of the board: it was the same dynamic at work. The avalanche of gangster films in 1931 and 1932 and the immense success of Warner's musicals demonstrate the pulling power of that dead model during the worst years of financial hardship. So the gang cycle emerges as less despairing and lawless than willfully optimistic: the nation going to the bottom of the social barrel before finding a credible vehicle for its success dreams. While Will Hays would have been happier without the gang films, they fit his definition of Hollywood's chief contributions to national stability more exactly than any other genre.

The shyster cycle was simply a diversion—the resurrection of a familiar scapegoat. As *Lawyer Man*'s William Powell returned to the Lower East Side to fight political bossism, who, in 1932, was being kidded? One suspects nearly everyone. It was another kind of reassurance. The gaping catastrophe was ignored and the terms of righteous indignation directed toward comprehensible, if fictitious, grounds. Dishonest ward heelers and lawyers obviously had little to do with the ongoing disaster of 1931–32, but at least they were visible. Hence the shyster cycle, like the gangster cycle, was less an expression of cynicism than an attempt to exercise a sense of control over what was wrong. The problem was that the figures and caricatures used and generated by this cycle were not symbolic, but irrelevant.

If the films produced before the New Deal seemed unable to even express what had happened to the country, unable to react except by cranking out familiar caricatures and dreams of individual achievement, it was understandable. Too much had been gutted too quickly for anything but an instinctive turning to corruption or success fantasies. "Melancholia and defeat," writes historian Irving Bernstein, "had overwhelmed not only the jobless but also those who sought to infuse spirit in them. Workers on their way down were in no mood to improve, far less to reorganize society." [3]

The evasions of the films of the mid-thirties, however, seem less excusable. "Back to the earth" was an early escape, although Vidor used it in *Our Daily Bread* in advocacy of cooperatives. But he was quite alone in depicting an alternative life-style, alone in his most implicit of hints that perhaps America need not be totally dedicated to fierce and enervating and dehumanizing competition for prescribed goals. But the mid-thirties mainly streamlined and reinforced the old goals. The topical films, the revival of cowboys, and the coming of G-Men films spoke automatically to the benevolence of federal law, which in turn was vanquishing bad men and releasing the old competitive energies in America. Hollywood constructed a government which it identified with justice and order, and which delivered the nation from external threats to its safety and industry. G-Men made the nation safe, as their predecessors on horseback had made the frontier a safe place for families to be raised. All this talk of G-Men, shysters, and entrepreneurship may seem diffuse and disconnected, about elements of a narrow vision limited to Hollywood, but Franklin Roosevelt synthesized them in a 1936 campaign speech:

Because kidnappers and bank robbers could in high-powered cars speed across state lines it became necessary, in order to protect our people, to invoke the power of the Federal Government. In the same way speculators and manipulators from across State lines, regardless of State laws, have lured the unsuspecting and the unwary to financial destruction. In the same way across State lines, there have been built up intricate corporate structures . . . huge monopolies which were stifling independent business and private enterprises.[4]

G-Man and trust-buster merged. But despite the talk about "intricate corporate structures" and "huge monopolies," the New Deal found itself unable to reconcile monopoly and democracy, vacillating between working with corporate concentration and breaking its power.[5] By the time the Temporary National Economic Committee again started probing the corporate stranglehold in 1938, it was far too late. The war would necessitate such concentration.

Epilogue: A New Set of Outlaws

In late 1967, when the federal government was farther removed from popular affections than at any time since 1932, *Bonnie And Clyde* arrived to engage public interest in a very significant way. Suddenly, people were fascinated by the thirties—clothing, hair styles, lingo—and once again attracted to outlaws. As before, when the state appeared to be willfully presiding over social collapse, the outlaw became a dynamic and tragic figure, one filled with contemporary meaning. No economic loss to breed a *Little Caesar* rags-to-riches saga in 1967: the problems of that year were subtle, varied, and more explosive than the simple, if awful, breakdown of the Great Depression. The apathy and melancholy of a people struck by economic helplessness was replaced by the anguish and activism of those struck by national ruthlessness. *Bonnie And Clyde* was released a scant two months before the anti-war march on the

Pentagon in October of 1967, and its distance from *Caesar* described the spectacular jolts to our sensibilities during the decades since Rico had soared to the top.

Director Arthur Penn's vision of the outlaw fit the sixties as exactly as Rico fit the thirties. Clyde had more roots in Freud than in Carnegie: sexually impotent and violent, his portrait brought together socio-psychological strains of the fifties and sixties. Rootless, homeless, anomic, Clyde is going toward nothing; he is just running from. "You better keep running, Clyde Barrow," says Bonnie's wizened mother. But where? Clyde aspires to no gang leadership: the cut and dried dynamics of the early thirties are replaced by a hodge-podge of sociological loose ends. It was Clyde's lack of focus as an outlaw that made him the darling of 1967, the bloodiness of his demise that made audiences somehow reach to him, puzzled at their reasons for doing so. If the Johnson government was the law, then increasing numbers of people knew they were outside it: outside its draft laws, outside the drug laws. For thousands, 1967 marked a watershed, marked their deepening sense of becoming outlaws.

Cool Hand Luke was also made in 1967—a chain gang film some ten years after the last chain gang had been abolished! But like *I Am A Fugitive . . .* , which it drew upon heavily, *Cool Hand Luke* had less to do with penal conditions than with the state as penal colony, in the mode of Kafka. The film's law was a prison guard wearing sun-glasses which reflected all, but the glasses concealed his eyes so thoroughly that one doubted he had them. Impenetrable, death-dealing and all-powerful, the guard stands above the prison gang. Again, *Cool Hand Luke*'s society was ages distant from that depicted in *I Am A Fugitive . . .* With success mechanisms still salient, James Allen escapes from the chain gang in order to work his way up and prove his worth. The emptiness of his society lay in its failure to provide economic security. Luke plays himself off against authority in an almost abstract fashion: his "crime" is taking the heads off parking meters, a destruction of public property which brings no financial gain, but which places him, almost formally, outside the law. The ways in which he attempts to gain his freedom and selfhood under impossible condi-

tions are at the core of the film. His outlawry is a state of mind—
the parking meter "caper" really harms no one—but it defines
his relationship to the society. Luke touched sixties concerns
deeply.

With *Easy Rider*, an endlessly flawed and endlessly attended
film, we have the ultimate coda to this study of Depression film-
making. No film would have been more unthinkable in the 1930s.

Unthinkable not for the obvious reasons—the long hair, the
marijuana smoke that practically wafted off the screen—but for
its premise: two outlaws desperately trying to escape success, and
re-defining success. They sell dope as much to establish their outlawry as for money, and having done that, they turn the success
mechanism inside out. For success becomes enmeshed not in hard
work and discipline, but in the absence of both. Where gangsters
of the thirties went through paces aimed at preserving everything
the state believed in—competition, power, money—outlaws of the
sixties were, literally and figuratively, something else.

"A man went looking for America," said the ad copy for *Easy
Rider*, "and couldn't find it anywhere." "We blew it," says Fonda,
at the end. They haven't found the peace they sought or new
land on which to settle. Fonda and Hopper are new kinds of
frontiersmen, going from west to east and attempting to escape
the logic of the old frontier, a frontier which in 1969 had ended
up in Asia. Physical and technical growth could be pursued no
longer: different kinds of growth were looked for.

So it is ironic that *Easy Rider* returns to an impulse of the
thirties by embracing a "back to the earth" escape from the nation's problems. When Fonda and Hopper visit a yeoman, they
tell him, with hokey reverence, "You're doing your own thing in
your own time," and then roar away on their motorcycles. They
visit a commune and watch the residents sowing seeds into very
unpromising soil. Again reverence: "They're going to make it,"
and again the two roar off. Somehow, in the process of "blowing
it," Hopper and Fonda know the "back to the earth" formula is
no answer for them. But what is? The two get killed off, in the
tradition of *Black Legion*, by a violent and ugly populace. In
the thirties, that violence would be controlled by a benevolent

government. But that solution no longer existed in the late sixties, when federal benevolence began to get ugly, began to rankle, began to overwhelm.

With redress to federal benevolence no longer possible and the law a sightless watchman, outlawry again seemed a legitimate stance in society. As in the gangster films, death was inevitable: Bonnie, Clyde, Luke, and the dope-dealing cyclists all lie dead at their picture's end. Unlike Depression gang heroes, the outlaws of the sixties were hard-pressed for a positive code. Indeed, they most resembled James Allen of *I Am A Fugitive* . . . in their stance of perpetual flight. Stopping meant settling, and that seemed quite impossible. As the 1970s began, uncertainty deepened and American films like *Joe* and even *Patton* seemed profoundly unsure as to who were the heroes and who were the villains. Definite answers were not forthcoming.

Notes

INTRODUCTION

1. *The 1935 Film Daily Year Book of Motion Pictures* (New York, 1935), p. 301.
2. *Exhibitors Herald-World*, November 19, 1929, p. 25.
3. *Motion Picture Herald*, January 2, 1932, p. 18.
4. Cf. Frederick Elkin, "Value Implications of Popular Films," *Sociology And Social Research*, May/June, 1954, p. 320.
5. Arthur Schlesinger, Jr., "When The Movies Really Counted," *Show*, April, 1963, p. 77.
6. James Agee, *Agee On Film, Reviews And Comments* (Boston, 1966 ed.), p. 41.
7. Siegfried Kracauer, *From Caligari to Hitler* (Princeton, 1966 ed.).
8. *Ibid.*, p. 5.
9. *Ibid.*
10. *Ibid.*
11. Franklin Fearing, "Films As History," *Hollywood Quarterly*, vol. II (1947), pp. 424–26.
12. Kracauer, *op. cit.*, p. 8.

13. Herbert Gans, "The Creator-Audience Relationship In The Mass Media: An Analysis Of Movie-Making," in Nathan Rosenberg and David White, *Mass Media* (Glencoe, 1957), p. 315.
14. Herbert Blumer, *Movies And Conduct* (New York, 1933), p. 116.

A NOTE ON THE MOVIE INDUSTRY AND THE DEPRESSION

1. *The 1935 Film Daily Year Book*, p. 301.
2. *Motion Picture Herald*, August 29, 1936, p. 15.
3. Lewis Jacobs, *The Rise of The American Film* (New York, 1939), p. 423.
4. *Motion Picture Herald*, November 9, 1929, p. 28; Adolph Zukor, *The Public Is Never Wrong* (New York, 1935), p. 261.
5. *The 1931 Film Daily Year Book Of Motion Pictures* (New York, 1931), p. 3.
6. *Ibid.*, p. 551.
7. *Motion Picture Herald*, January 17, 1931, p. 49; October 24, 1931, p. 9.
8. *The 1932 Film Daily Year Book Of Motion Pictures* (New York, 1932), p. 3.
9. *Motion Picture Herald*, August 29, 1936, p. 15.
10. Advertisement reprinted in *Motion Picture Herald*, November 14, 1932.
11. *The 1932 Film Daily Year Book Of Motion Pictures*, p. 39.
12. "Came The (Movie) Dawn," *Business Week*, November 9, 1935, p. 78.
13. *The 1933 Film Daily Year Book of Motion Pictures* (New York, 1933), p. 3.
14. *Ibid.*, p. 91.
15. *Motion Picture Herald*, October 14, 1933, p. 23; April 8, 1933, p. 8.
16. *The 1934 Film Daily Year Book Of Motion Pictures* (New York, 1934), p. 3; *Motion Picture Herald*, August 29, 1936, p. 15.
17. "Bank Night," *Time*, February 3, 1936, p. 58; Forbes Parkhill, "Bank Night Tonight," *Saturday Evening Post*, December 4, 1937, pp. 20–21.
18. Gilbert Seldes, "The Quicksands of the Movies," *Atlantic Monthly*, October, 1936, p. 423.
19. *The 1935 Film Daily Year Book Of Motion Pictures* (New York, 1935), p. 3; *Business Week*, "Movies Hit Prosperity Trail," November 21, 1936, p. 22.

THE GANGSTERS

1. Arthur Knight, *The Liveliest Art* (New York, 1957), p. 238.
2. Will Hays, *The President's Report to the Motion Picture Producers And Distributors of America* (New York, 1932), pp. 21–22; *Motion Picture Herald*, April 11, 1931, p. 43; Interstate And Foreign Commerce Committee, *Hearings On H.R. 6097, To Create A Federal Motion Picture Commission*, 73rd Congress, 2nd Session (1934), p. 16.
3. *Ibid.*, pp. 18, 34.
4. *The Commonweal*, June 10, 1931, pp. 143–44; Alexander Bashky, "The Underworld," *The Nation*, January 21, 1931, p. 8.
5. Walter B. Pitkin, "Screen Crime Vs. Press Crime," *The Outlook*, July 29, 1931, pp. 398, 414.
6. *The Christian Century*, August 12, 1931, p. 1015; A. Edmund Williamson, "Ridding Local Movies Of Gangster Films," *The American City*, September, 1931, pp. 112–13.
7. Will Hays, *The Memoirs Of Will Hays* (Garden City, 1955), pp. 433–34; *Motion Picture Herald*, April 4, 1930, p. 12.
8. *Film Daily*, February 6, 1931, p. 1.
9. Will Hays, *The President's Report* . . . (New York, 1932), pp. 21–22.
10. Warner Brothers press sheet, *Little Caesar* (New York, 1930).
11. Dwight MacDonald, "Notes On Hollywood Directors, Part II," *Symposium*, July, 1933, pp. 293–94.
12. "The Road To Business Success, An Address To Young Men," in Andrew Carnegie, *The Empire Of Business* (New York, 1917), p. 1.
13. *Ibid.*, pp. 4–5.
14. Edward G. Robinson, "The Movie, The Actor and Public Morals," in William J. Perlman (ed.), *The Movies On Trial* (New York, 1936), pp. 28–29.
15. W. R. Burnett, *Little Caesar* (New York, 1929), p. 134.
16. Carnegie, *op. cit.*, pp. 17–18; Burnett, *op. cit.*, p. 162.
17. Carnegie, *op. cit.*, p. 11.
18. *Ibid.*, p. 13.
19. *Ibid.*, pp. 13–14.
20. Robert Warshow, "The Gangster As Tragic Hero," in *The Immediate Experience* (New York, 1964 ed.), p. 88.
21. Lincoln Kirstein, "James Cagney And The American Hero," *Hound And Horn*, April/June, 1932, pp. 466–67.

22. *The New York Times*, April 24, 1931.
23. John Keats, *Howard Hughes* (New York, 1966), pp. 52–54.
24. MGM press sheet, *The Secret Six* (New York, 1931).
25. United Artists press sheet, *Corsair* (New York, 1931).
26. Paul Rotha and Richard Griffith, *The Film Till Now* (New York, 1951 ed.), pp. 435–36.
27. *Ibid.*, pp. 436–37.
28. Edgar Dale, *The Content Of Motion Pictures* (New York, 1933), p. 130.
29. The gangster as individual entrepreneur was changing in fact as well as on film. In 1934, mobster Johnny Torrio (who had given Al Capone his Chicago start) convinced top gang leaders that unity meant strength. Competition between gangs slowed and the Syndicate emerged. Burton Turkus and Sid Feder, *Murder, Inc.* (New York, 1951), pp. 96–100.
30. Warshow, *op. cit.*, p. 86.

THE SHYSTER AND THE CITY

1. "What Is America?" *The Nation*, June 26, 1929, p. 75.
2. *Ibid.*; Anselm Strauss, *Images Of The American City* (Glencoe, 1961), pp. 121–22.
3. Ford Maddox Ford, *New York Is Not America* (New York, 1927), p. 95.
4. Phillip Stong, *State Fair* (New York, 1932), p. 149; *The Nation, op. cit.*; "Unsavory Conditions," *The Commonweal*, August 5, 1931, p. 333; "They Hate New York," *The New Republic*, May 20, 1931, pp. 4–5; Elmer Davis, "Our Island Universe," *Harper's Magazine*, November, 1929, pp. 680–692; Earl Sparling, "Is New York American?" *Scribner's*, August, 1931, pp. 165–73.
5. Stanley Walker, *City Editor* (New York, 1934), pp. 4–7.
6. St. Clair McKelway, *Gossip, The Life And Times Of Walter Winchell* (New York, 1940), pp. 15–18.
7. Lewis Mumford, "From A City Notebook," *The New Republic*, September 18, 1929, p. 125.
8. Sparling, *op. cit.*
9. MGM press sheet, *Washington Merry-Go-Round* (New York, 1932).
10. A. Fenner Brockway, *Can Roosevelt Succeed?* (London, 1934), p. 252.
11. Irving Bernstein, *The Lean Years* (Baltimore, 1966 ed.), pp. 435–36; Schlesinger, *The Crisis Of The Old Order* (Boston, 1957), p. 252.

12. Bernstein, *op. cit.*, p. 416.
13. Warner Brothers press sheet, *The Mouthpiece* (New York, 1932).
14. George S. Kaufman and Morris Ryskind, *Of Thee I Sing* (New York, 1958 ed.), p. 17.
15. MGM press sheet, *Washington Masquerade* (New York, 1932).
16. Bosley Crowther, *Hollywood Rajah* (New York, 1960), p. 178.

Some Anarcho-Nihilist Laff Riots

1. Will Hays, *Annual Report To The Motion Picture Producers and Distributors of America* (New York, 1934), p. 2.
2. Jesse Lasky, *I Blow My Own Horn* (New York, 1957), p. 228.
3. Antonin Artaud, *The Theatre And Its Double* (New York, 1958), pp. 142–44.
4. *Ibid.*
5. *Motion Picture Herald*, September 6, 1930, pp. 38–39.
6. *Ibid.*, July 2, 1932, p. 40.
7. *Ibid.*, August 29, 1932, pp. 22–23.
8. New York *Herald-Tribune*, November 24, 1933.
9. *The New York Times*, November 24, 1933.
10. William Troy, "Films," *The Nation*, December 13, 1933, p. 688.
11. Allen Eyles, *The Marx Brothers: Their World Of Comedy* (London, 1966), p. 86.
12. *Motion Picture Herald*, April 7, 1934; December 23, 1933, p. 62; March 3, 1934, p. 58.
13. Martin Esslin, *The Theatre Of The Absurd* (New York, 1961), p. 237; Agee, *op. cit.*, p. 17.
14. Robert Lewis Taylor, *W. C. Fields, His Follies And Fortunes* (New York, 1967 ed.), pp. 18–20.
15. William K. Everson, *The Art Of W. C. Fields* (New York, 1967), p. 85.

Sex and Personal Relations

1. Jane Addams, *A New Conscience And An Ancient Evil* (New York, 1912), p. 78; "Poverty Breeding Vice," *The Literary Digest*, January 9, 1932, p. 22; Adolph Zukor, *The Public Is Never Wrong* (New York, 1953), p. 267.
2. Rotha and Griffith, *op. cit.*, pp. 438–39.
3. MGM press sheet, *Faithless* (New York, 1932).
4. In 1933, it was estimated by the National Committee on the Care of the Transient and Homeless that at least 75,000 women were

without shelter. Henrietta S. Ripperger, "The Forgotten Woman," *Ladies Home Journal*, August, 1933, p. 24.

5. The bureau of missing persons figured in a number of early thirties films, and in 1933 Warner Brothers released a fine Pat O'Brien/ Bette Davis comedy called *Bureau Of Missing Persons*. The bureau was a kind of grim and sardonic scoreboard, chalking up society's dropouts.

6. *Motion Picture Herald*, February 3, 1934, pp. 16–17.

7. *Ibid.*, March 11, 1933, p. 36; June 17, 1933, p. 48.

8. Gilbert Seldes, *The Movies Come From America* (New York, 1937), p. 35.

9. Knight, *op. cit.*, p. 151; Kracauer, *From Caligari To Hitler*, pp. 23–24, 55–65.

10. *Ibid.*, p. 57.

11. Dwight MacDonald, "Notes On Hollywood Directors, Part I," *Symposium*, April, 1933, pp. 170–72.

12. *Motion Picture Herald*, December 2, 1933, p. 45.

13. *Ibid.*, December 2, 1933, p. 45.

14. *Ibid.*, February 3, 1934, p. 69.

15. "The Confused Generation," *Scribner's*, January, 1932, pp. 50–53.

16. Schlesinger, "When The Movies Really Counted," *op. cit.*, p. 125.

A Musical Interlude

1. *The 1934 Film Daily Year Book Of Motion Pictures*, p. 89.

2. *Motion Picture Herald*, February 3, 1934, pp. 16–17.

3. *Ibid.*, February 6, 1937, p. 63.

Back to the Earth: King Kong and King Vidor

1. *Motion Picture Herald*, June 17, 1933, p. 48.

2. Arthur Schlesinger, Jr., *The Coming Of The New Deal* (Boston, 1959), p. 362; Paul Conkin, *Tomorrow A New World* (Ithaca, 1959), p. 81.

3. George Mowry and Judson Grenier, introduction to David Graham Phillips, *The Treason Of The Senate* (Chicago, 1964), pp. 11–12.

4. Schlesinger, *The Coming Of The New Deal*, p. 362; Twelve Southerners, *I'll Take My Stand* (New York, 1962 ed.), p. 152.

5. *Motion Picture Herald*, January 6, 1934, p. 15; August 16, 1932, p. 10.

6. MacDonald, "Notes On Directors, Part I," *op. cit.*, pp. 176–77.

7. Lewis Atherton, *Main Street On The Middle Border* (Bloomington, 1954), p. 252.
8. MacDonald, *op. cit.*
9. Bosley Crowther, *The Great Films* (New York, 1967), p. 97.
10. King Vidor, *A Tree Is A Tree* (New York, 1953), pp. 146, 220.
11. *Ibid.*
12. *Ibid.*, p. 146.
13. C. Wright Mills, *White Collar* (New York, 1951).
14. Vidor, *op. cit.*, pp. 152–53.
15. Quoted in Page Smith, *As A City Upon A Hill* (New York, 1966), p. 8.
16. Vidor, *op. cit.*, pp. 221–27.
17. *Ibid.*
18. *Motion Picture Herald*, August 18, 1934, p. 38; Andre Sennewald, "King Vidor And Our Daily Bread," *The New York Times*, October 7, 1934; William Troy, "Collectivism More Or Less," *The Nation*, June 24, 1934, p. 493; Peter Ellis, "Let's Build A Ditch," *The New Masses*, October 6, 1934, p. 30.
19. Page Smith, *op. cit.*
20. Schlesinger, *The Coming Of The New Deal*, pp. 363–64.
21. *Ibid.*, p. 371; Robert and Helen Merrell Lynd, *Middletown In Transition* (New York, 1937), pp. 116, 135.
22. *Motion Picture Herald*, January 5, 1935, p. 61; February 16, 1935, p. 75.

THE G-MAN AND THE COWBOY

1. *Motion Picture Herald*, July 13, 1935, p. 36.
2. Will Hays, *The President's Report* . . . (New York, 1936).
3. August Vollmer, *The Police And Modern Society* (Berkeley: 1936), pp. 3–4; "G-Men Wage Unending War," *The Literary Digest*, August 3, 1935, p. 18.
4. *Motion Picture Herald*, April 24, 1935, p. 3; May 1, 1935, p. 3; Warner Brothers Campaign Book, *G-Men* (New York, 1935).
5. *Motion Picture Herald*, July 27, 1935, p. 73; *Newsweek*, May 2, 1936, p. 13.
6. *Time*, June 1, 1936, p. 26.
7. Warner Brothers press sheet, *Bullets Or Ballots* (New York, 1936).
8. *Motion Picture Herald*, April 1, 1933, p. 9.
9. *Ibid.*

10. *Ibid.*, May 16, 1936, p. 38; November 9, 1935, p. 3; George F. Fenin and William K. Everson, *The Western* (New York, 1962), p. 204.
11. Milton Mayer, "The Myth of the G-Man," *The Forum*, September, 1935, p. 145.
12. Cf. Henry Nash Smith, *Virgin Land* (New York, 1950), pp. 54–98.
13. *Motion Picture Herald*, June 15, 1937, p. 60.

WARNER BROTHERS PRESENTS SOCIAL CONSCIOUSNESS

1. *Motion Picture Herald*, November 19, 1932, pp. 20–21; December 17, 1932, pp. 20–21.
2. *Ibid.*, June 21, 1930, p. 55.
3. *Ibid.*, March 11, 1933, p. 62.
4. Peter Ellis, "Movies," *The New Masses*, April 23, 1935, pp. 28–29.
5. Jack Warner, *My First Hundred Years In Hollywood* (New York, 1965), pp. 290–94.
6. Rotha and Griffith, *op. cit.*, p. 442.
7. Richard Watts, Jr., in New York *Herald-Tribune*, July 22, 1933.
8. *Ibid.*
9. *Motion Picture Herald*, May 27, 1933, p. 32.
10. Estimates of the number of transients in 1932–1933 ranged as high as two million, and most studies claimed that one fourth of these were people under the age of 21. Schlesinger, *The Crisis Of The Old Order*, p. 251; A. Wayne McMillen, "An Army of Boys On The Loose," *Survey*, September, 1932, p. 389; Carmen Haider, *Do We Want Fascism?* (New York, 1934), p. 154.
11. William Troy, "Forgotten Children," *The Nation*, October 18, 1934, p. 458.
12. William K. Everson, program notes for "The Depression: Two Films by William Wellman," The New School for Social Research, October 27, 1967.
13. Troy, "Forgotten Children," *op. cit.*
14. *Motion Picture Herald*, May 27, 1932, p. 32.
15. *Ibid.*, September 30, 1933, p. 40.
16. William K. Everson, program notes for "Political Comment: Satire and Melodrama," The New School for Social Research, October 13, 1967.
17. Ellis, "Movies," *op. cit.*
18. *Motion Picture Herald*, April 13, 1935, p. 18.
19. *Ibid.*, April 6, 1935, pp. 18, 26; Otis Ferguson, "Men Working," *The New Republic*, April 24, 1935, p. 313.

20. Ellis, "Movies," *op. cit.*; Andre Sennewald, "Coal Mine Melo-drama," *The New York Times*, April 7, 1935; *The Literary Digest*, April 27, 1935, p. 34.

THE MOB AND THE SEARCH FOR AUTHORITY, 1933–1937

1. *See, for instance,* A. Fenner Brockway, *Will Roosevelt Succeed?* (London, 1934); George Sokolsky, "America Drifts Toward Fascism," *The American Mercury*, July, 1934, p. 259; Raymond Gram Swing, *Forerunners Of American Fascism* (New York, 1935), pp. 13–14; Schlesinger, *The Crisis Of The Old Order*, p. 268.
2. Lawrence Dennis, *The Coming American Fascism* (New York, 1936); Travis Hoke, *Shirts! A Survey* . . . (New York, 1934), p. 3; Schlesinger, *The Politics Of Upheaval* (Boston, 1960), pp. 74–86.
3. T. Harry Williams, *Huey Long* (New York, 1969).
4. Schlesinger, *The Crisis Of The Old Order*, pp. 460–61.
5. Paramount press sheet, *This Day And Age* (New York, 1933).
6. Sinclair Lewis, *It Can't Happen Here* (New York, 1935), p. 67.
7. George Mosse (ed.), *Nazi Culture* (New York, 1966), pp. 290–91.
8. *Ibid.*, p. 261.
9. *Ibid.*, pp. 32–34; Donald Hayne (ed.), *The Autobiography Of Cecil B. DeMille* (Englewood Cliffs, 1959), pp. 236–37.
10. Milton Mayer, "The Myth Of The G-Man," *op. cit.*
11. *The Autobiography Of Cecil B. DeMille*, pp. 326–27.
12. *Motion Picture Herald*, August 29, 1933, p. 28.
13. Schlesinger, *The Crisis Of The Old Order*, p. 268.
14. *Motion Picture Herald*, October 7, 1933, p. 52; November 4, 1933, p. 45; November 18, 1933, p. 57.
15. Kracauer, *From Caligari To Hitler*, p. 225.
16. "A President After Hollywood's Heart," *The Literary Digest*, April 22, 1933, p. 13; Schlesinger, *The Crisis Of The Old Order*, pp. 460–61.
17. Crowther, *Hollywood Rajah*, pp. 178–80.
18. Lewis, *It Can't Happen Here*, pp. 78–79.
19. Schlesinger, *The Crisis Of The Old Order*, pp. 460–61.
20. Lewis, *It Can't Happen Here*, pp. 248–49.
21. Milton Mayer denounced "the spirit that seeks order at the expense of justice. It embraces the creation of police armies to fight crime, with the general view that police armies may be put to a number of uses." "The Myth of the G-Man," *op. cit.*, p. 146.
22. Creighton Peet, "Politics On The Screen," *Stage*, May, 1933, p. 42.

23. *Motion Picture Herald*, July 19, 1933, p. 52; May 20, 1933; August 12, 1933, p. 56.

24. William Troy, "Fascism Over Hollywood," *The Nation*, April 26, 1933, pp. 482–83; Stark Young, "Gabriel's Horn," *The New Republic*, April 19, 1933, p. 281.

25. Schlesinger, *The Politics Of Upheaval*, p. 95.

26. Troy, "Fascism Over Hollywood," *op. cit.*

27. Lang fled Germany after a 1933 meeting with Nazi propaganda chieftain Josef Goebbels. Lang recollects: "He said to me, 'The Fuhrer has seen your pictures and he has said "This is the man who will give us the big Nazi pictures." ' " Andrew Sarris (ed.), *Interviews With Film Directors* (Indianapolis, 1967), p. 260.

28. *The Literary Digest*, August 1, 1936, p. 32; NAACP, *Can The States Stop Lynching?* (New York, 1937); Schlesinger, *The Politics Of Upheaval*, pp. 436–38.

29. *The New Republic*, July 28, 1937, p. 335.

30. Exhibitors Campaign Book, *Fury* (New York, 1936).

31. Peter Bogdanovich, *Fritz Lang In America* (New York, 1969), pp. 27–28.

FRANK CAPRA AND SCREWBALL COMEDY, 1931–1941

1. Richard Griffith, "Frank Capra," *British Film Institute*, New Index Series, no. 3, 1951, p. 6.

2. Frank Capra, "Sacred Cows To The Slaughter," *Stage*, July, 1936, p. 41.

3. Quoted in Knight, *The Liveliest Art*, pp. 241–42.

4. *Ibid.*, p. 241.

5. Alva Johnston, "Capra Shoots As He Pleases," *Saturday Evening Post*, May 14, 1938, p. 8; Griffith, "Frank Capra," *op. cit.*, p. 6.

6. *Ibid.*

7. Cf. Bob Thomas, *King Cohn* (New York, 1967).

8. Griffith, "Frank Capra," *op. cit.*, p. 15.

9. Not being able to locate a print of *Lady For A Day*, I was forced to base my analysis on a reading of the script, located in the Theatre Collection of the New York Public Library.

10. Capra, "Sacred Cows To The Slaughter," *op. cit.*

11. Barbara Deming, "The Library Of Congress Film Project: Exposition of a Method," *Library of Congress Quarterly*, November, 1944, p. 26.

12. Robert Stebbins, "Mr. Capra Goes To Town," *New Theatre*, May, 1936, p. 17.
13. Robert and Helen Merrell Lynd, *Middletown In Transition*, pp. 446–47.
14. Deming, "The Library of Congress Film Project," *op. cit.*
15. Robert Stebbins, *New Theatre*, November, 1936, p. 22; F. Scott Fitzgerald, "The Rich Boy," in *Babylon Revisited And Other Stories* (New York, 1960 ed.), p. 152.
16. Crowther, *The Great Films*, p. 102.
17. William Troy, "On A Classic," *The Nation*, April 10, 1935, pp. 416–17.
18. Thomas, *King Cohn*, p. 121.
19. Griffith, "Frank Capra," *op. cit.*, pp. 4, 21.
20. *Motion Picture Herald*, May 30, 1936, pp. 44–45; June 17, 1936, pp. 30–31; August 15, 1936, p. 69; November 28, 1936, p. 91.
21. Griffith, "Frank Capra," *op. cit.*, p. 14.
22. *Ibid.*, p. 22; Stebbins, "Mr. Capra Goes To Town," *op. cit.*, pp. 17–18.
23. Geoffrey Hellman, "Thinker In Hollywood," *The New Yorker*, February 24, 1940, p. 29.
24. *Ibid.*, pp. 23–24.
25. Warshow, *op. cit.*, p. 86.
26. Hellman, "Thinker In Hollywood," *op. cit.*, p. 28.

A SOLUTION TO ENVIRONMENT: THE JUVENILE DELINQUENT

1. Edgar Dale, *op. cit.*, p. 130.
2. Warshow, *op. cit.*, p. 86.
3. Roy Lubove, *The Progressives And The Slums* (Pittsburgh, 1962), pp. 6–7, 47, 174, 255.
4. T. Earl Sullenger, *Social Determinants In Juvenile Delinquency* (New York, 1936), p. 6.
5. William Healy and Augusta Brommer, *New Light On Delinquency And Its Treatment* (New Haven, 1936), p. 28.
6. "Busting Gangs As They Blossom," *The Literary Digest*, May 29, 1937, p. 19.
7. Edith Abbott, *The Tenements Of Chicago* (Chicago, 1936), pp. 494–95; J. Joseph Huthmacher, *Senator Robert F. Wagner And The Rise Of Urban Liberalism* (New York, 1968), pp. 205–30.
8. Morgan Himelstein, *Drama Was A Weapon* (New Brunswick, 1963), pp. 197–98.

9. *Life,* August 30, 1937, pp. 62–63.
10. Warner Brothers press sheet, *The Mayor Of Hell* (New York, 1933).
11. United Artists press sheet, *Dead End* (New York, 1937).
12. *See* Alfred Kazin's wonderful *Starting Out In The Thirties* (Boston, 1965) for an evocation of this world.
13. *See* Jane Jacobs', *The Life And Death Of Great American Cities* (New York, 1961) for a brilliant discussion of the relation of active streets to a vital and human city.
14. Clifford Shaw, *Delinquency Areas* (Chicago, 1929), p. 205.
15. Robert Gordon, "Issues In The Ecological Study of Delinquency," *American Sociological Review,* December, 1967. Gordon disagrees and sees a high correlation between extreme poverty and delinquency. But current disaffections among the young can hardly be studied in classic terms of "delinquency."
16. *Motion Picture Herald,* April 23, 1938, p. 64.
17. Himelstein, *Drama Was A Weapon,* pp. 197–98.
18. Bogdanovich, *Fritz Lang In America,* p. 35.
19. *See* Pauline Kael's comparison of the two films in *Kiss Kiss Bang Bang* (New York, 1968).
20. W. L. White, "Pare Lorentz," *Scribner's,* January, 1939, p. 9.

CONCLUSIONS

1. Will Hays, *Annual Report* . . . (New York, 1934), p. 2.
2. *The Public Papers And Addresses of Franklin D. Roosevelt,* V (New York, 1936), pp. 386, 389–90.
3. Bernstein, *The Lean Years,* pp. 435–36.
4. *The Public Papers And Addresses* . . . , p. 483.
5. See Ellis Hawley, *The New Deal and the Problem of Monopoly* (Princeton, 1966) for a masterful survey of the problem.

Bibliography

The Films

Alice Adams
Angel
Angels With Dirty Faces
Animal Crackers
The Awful Truth
Black Fury
Black Legion
Blonde Venus
Bullets Or Ballots
Bureau Of Missing Persons
City Streets
The Cocoanuts
Corsair
Crime School
The Crowd
Dames
The Dark Horse
Day At The Races

Dead End
Design For Living
The Devil Is A Sissy
Dinner At Eight
Duck Soup
Easy Living
Faithless
The Fatal Glass Of Beer
Footlight Parade
42nd Street
The Front Page
Fury
G-Men
Gabriel Over The White House
Goin To Town
Gold Diggers Of 1933
Gold Diggers Of 1935
Gold Diggers Of 1937

Gold Diggers Of Paris
The Great O'Malley
Hallelujah
Hell's Highway
Her Man
Heroes For Sale
Horsefeathers
I Am A Fugitive From A Chain
  Gang
I'm No Angel
It Happened One Night
It's A Gift
King Kong
Lady Killer
The Last Gangster
Lawyer Man
The Life Of Jimmy Dolan
Little Caesar
Little Giant
Lonesome
Lost Horizon
Marked Woman
Massacre
The Mayor Of Hell
Meet John Doe
Million Dollar Legs
Mr. Deeds Goes To Town
Mr. Smith Goes To Washington
The Mouthpiece
My Man Godfrey

A Night At The Opera
Nothing Sacred
One Hour With You
Our Daily Bread
The Petrified Forest
The Phantom President
The Plainsman
Platinum Blonde
The Plow That Broke The Plains
The President Vanishes
Professional Sweetheart
The Public Enemy
Public Enemy's Wife
Safe In Hell
Scandal Sheet
The Secret Six
She Done Him Wrong
State's Attorney
Susan Lenox, Her Fall And Rise
Taxi
The Texas Rangers
They Won't Forget
This Day And Age
Trouble In Paradise
The Virginian
Washington Masquerade
Wild Boys Of The Road
You Can't Take It With You
You Only Live Once

BOOKS AND ARTICLES

Abbott, Edith. *The Slums Of Chicago, 1909–1935*. Chicago, 1936.

Addams, Jane. *A New Conscience And An Ancient Evil*. New York, 1932.

Agee, James. *Agee On Film, Reviews And Comments*. Boston, 1966 ed.

Artaud, Antonin. *The Theatre And Its Double*. New York, 1958 ed.

Atherton, Lewis. *Main Street On The Middle Border*. Bloomington, 1954.

Berelson, Bernard. *Content Analysis In Communications Research.* Glencoe, 1952.

Bernstein, Irving. *The Lean Years.* Baltimore, 1966 ed.

Blumer, Herbert. *Movies And Conduct.* New York, 1933.

Bogdanovich, Peter. *Fritz Lang In America.* New York, 1969.

Branch, Douglas. *The Cowboy And His Interpreters.* New York, 1926.

Brockway, A. Fenner. *Will Roosevelt Succeed? A Study Of Fascist Tendencies In America.* London, 1934.

Burnett, W. R. *Little Caesar.* New York, 1929.

Business Week. "Came The (Movie) Dawn" (November 9, 1935).

————. "Movies Hit Prosperity Trail" (November 21, 1936).

Capra, Frank. "Sacred Cows To The Slaughter." *Stage.* July, 1936.

Carnegie, Andrew. *The Empire Of Business.* Garden City, 1917.

The Commonweal. "Gang Films." June 10, 1931.

————. "Unsavory Conditions." August 5, 1931.

Conkin, Paul. *Tomorrow A New World.* Ithaca, 1959.

Crowther, Bosley. *Hollywood Rajah.* New York, 1960.

————. *The Great Films.* New York, 1967.

Dale, Edgar. *The Content Of Motion Pictures.* New York, 1933.

Davis, Elmer. "Our Island Universe." *Harper's* (November, 1929).

Davy, Charles (ed.). *Footnotes To The Film.* London, 1937.

Deming, Barbara. "The Library Of Congress Film Project: Exposition Of A Method." *The Library Of Congress Quarterly Journal Of Current Acquisitions* (November, 1944).

Elkin, Frederick. "The Psychological Appeal Of The Hollywood Western." *Journal Of Educational Psychology* (1950).

————. "Value Implications Of Popular Films." *Sociology And Social Research* (May/June, 1954).

Ellis, Peter. "Let's Build A Ditch." *The New Masses* (October 16, 1934).

————. "Movies." *The New Masses* (April 23, 1935).

————. "The March Of Time." *The New Masses* (July 9, 1935).

Everson, William K. *The Art Of W. C. Fields.* New York, 1967.

Fearing, Franklin. "Films As History." *Hollywood Quarterly,* vol. II (1947).

Fenin, George F., and Everson, William K. *The Western.* New York, 1962.

Ferguson, Otis. "Cops And Robbers." *The New Republic* (May 15, 1935).

————. "Men Working." *The New Republic* (April 24, 1935).

————. "New Film In A Dry Month." *The New Republic* (July 28, 1937).

Ford, Ford Maddox. *New York Is Not America*. New York, 1927.

Gordon, Robert. "Issues In The Ecological Study Of Delinquency." *American Sociological Review* (December, 1967).

Griffith, Richard. "Frank Capra." *British Film Institute*, New Index Series, no. 3 (1951).

Haider, Carmen. *Do We Want Fascism?* New York, 1934.

Hawley, Ellis. *The New Deal and the Problem of Monopoly*. Princeton, 1966.

Hayne, Donald (ed.). *The Autobiography Of Cecil B. DeMille*. Englewood Cliffs, 1959.

Hays, Will H. *The Memoirs Of Will H. Hays*. Garden City, 1955.

————. *President's Report To The Motion Picture Producers And Distributors Of America*. New York, 1932.

————. *President's Report . . .* (New York, 1934).

Healy, William, and Bronner, Augusta. *New Light On Delinquency And Its Treatment*. New Haven, 1936.

Hellman, Geoffrey. "Thinker In Hollywood." *The New Yorker* (February 24, 1940).

Himelstein, Morgan. *Drama Was A Weapon*. New Brunswick, 1963.

Hoke, Travis. *Shirts! A survey of the new "Shirt" organizations in the United States seeking a Fascist dictatorship*. New York, 1934.

Huthmacher, J. Joseph. *Senator Robert F. Wagner And The Rise Of Urban Liberalism*. New York, 1968.

Jacobs, Lewis. *The Rise Of The American Film*. New York, 1939.

Johnston, Alva. "Capra Shoots As He Pleases." *The Saturday Evening Post* (May 14, 1938).

Kael, Pauline. *Kiss Kiss Bang Bang*. New York, 1968.

Kazin, Alfred. *Starting Out In The Thirties*. Boston, 1965.

Keats, John. *Howard Hughes*. New York, 1966.

Kempton, Murray. *Part Of Our Time*. New York, 1967 ed.

Kirstein, Lincoln. "James Cagney And The American Hero." *Hound And Horn* (April/June, 1932).

Kracauer, Siegfried. *From Caligari To Hitler*. Princeton, 1966 ed.

Krutch, Joseph Wood. "In Defense Of Mae West." *The Nation* (September 30, 1931).

Lahue, Kalton C. *World Of Laughter*. Norman, 1966.

Lasky, Jesse. *I Blow My Own Horn*. New York, 1957.

The Literary Digest. "Are Gang Films Wholesome?" (March 4, 1933).

————. "A President After Hollywood's Heart" (April 22, 1933).

————. "Combatting Mobs" (August 1, 1936).

————. " 'G-Men' Wage Unending War" (August 3, 1935).

————. "Poverty Breeding Vice" (January 9, 1932).

Lubove, Roy. *The Progressives And The Slums.* Pittsburgh, 1962.

Lynd, Robert S. and Helen Merrell. *Middletown In Transition.* New York, 1937.

MacDonald, Dwight. "Notes On Hollywood Directors, Parts I & II." *Symposium* (April–July, 1933).

McKelway, St. Clair. *Gossip, The Life And Times Of Walter Winchell.* New York, 1940.

Matthews, Jane DeHart. *The Federal Theatre, 1935–1939.* Princeton, 1967.

Mayer, Milton. "The Myth of the G-Man." *Forum* (September, 1935).

Mitchell, Broadus. *Depression Decade.* New York, 1947.

Moley, Raymond. *The Hays Office.* Indianapolis, 1945.

Mosse, George L. *Nazi Culture.* New York, 1966.

Motion Picture Herald (1929–1939 complete).

Mumford, Lewis. "From A City Notebook." *The New Republic* (September 18, 1929).

NAACP. *Can The States Stop Lynching?* New York, 1937.

The Nation. "What Is America?" (June 26, 1929).

The New Republic. "The Great Fascist Plot" (December 5, 1934).

————. "They Hate New York" (May 20, 1931).

Parkhill, Forbes. "Bank Night Tonight." *The Saturday Evening Post* (December 4, 1937).

Peet, Creighton. "Films Of The Year." *Stage* (July, 1933).

————. "Politics On The Screen." *Stage* (May, 1933).

Perlman, William (ed.). *The Movies On Trial.* New York, 1936.

Pitkin, Walter B. "Screen Crime Vs. Press Crime." *The Outlook* (July 29, 1931).

Prentice, Frances Woodward. "The Confused Generation." *Scribner's* (January, 1932).

Review Of Reviews. "Contrasts In The Life Of A City" (April, 1931).

Ripperger, Henrietta. "The Forgotten Woman." *Ladies Home Journal* (August, 1933).

Roosevelt, Franklin D. *The Public Papers And Addresses Of Franklin D. Roosevelt.* Volume V. New York, 1938.

Rosenberg, Nathan, and White, David. *Mass Culture*. Glencoe, 1957.

Rosten, Leo. *Hollywood*. New York, 1941.

Rotha, Paul, and Griffith, Richard. *The Film Till Now*. New York, 1951 ed.

──────. *Documentary Film*. London, 1957.

Sarris, Andrew (ed.). *Interviews With Film Directors*. Indianapolis, 1967.

Schlesinger, Arthur, Jr. *The Crisis Of The Old Order*. Boston, 1957.

──────. *The Coming Of The New Deal*. Boston, 1959.

──────. *The Politics Of Upheaval*. Boston, 1960.

──────. "When The Movies Really Counted." *Show* (April, 1963).

Seldes, Gilbert. *The Movies Come From America*. New York, 1937.

──────. "The Quicksands Of The Movies." *Atlantic Monthly* (October, 1936).

──────. *The Seven Lively Arts*. New York, 1962 ed.

Sennewald, Andre. "Coal Mine Melodrama." *The New York Times* (April 7, 1935).

──────. "King Vidor And Our Daily Bread." *The New York Times* (October 7, 1934).

Shaw, Clifford. *Delinquency Areas*. Chicago, 1929.

Smith, Henry Nash. *Virgin Land*. New York, 1950.

Smith, Page. *As A City Upon A Hill*. New York, 1966.

Sokolsky, George. "America Drifts Toward Fascism." *The American Mercury* (July, 1934).

Sparling, Earl. "Is New York American?" *Scribner's* (August, 1931).

Stebbins, Robert. "Mr. Capra Goes To Town." *New Theatre* (May, 1936).

Stong, Phillip. *State Fair*. New York, 1932.

Strauss, Anselm. *Images Of The American City*. Glencoe, 1961.

Sullenger, T. Earl. *Social Determinants In Juvenile Delinquency*. New York, 1936.

Swing, Raymond Gram. *Forerunners Of American Fascism*. New York, 1935.

Talbot, Daniel (ed.). *Film: An Anthology*. New York, 1959.

Thomas, Bob. *King Cohn*. New York, 1967.

Time Magazine. "Bank Night" (February 3, 1936).

Troy, William. "Collectivism More Or Less." *The Nation* (October 24, 1934).

──────. "Fascism Over Hollywood." *The Nation* (April 26, 1933).

──────. "Forgotten Children." *The Nation* (October 18, 1933).

————. "On A Classic." *The Nation* (April 10, 1935).

Turkus, Burton, and Feder, Sid. *Murder, Inc.* New York, 1951.

Twelve Southerners. *I'll Take My Stand.* New York, 1962 ed.

Tyler, Parker. *The Hollywood Hallucination.* New York, 1944.

United States, Interstate and Foreign Commerce Committee, House of Representatives. *Hearings On H.R. 6097, To Create A Federal Motion Picture Commission,* 73rd Congress, 2nd Session, 1934.

Vidor, King. *A Tree Is A Tree.* New York, 1953.

Von Sternberg, Josef. *Fun In A Chinese Laundry.* New York, 1965.

Wagenknecht, Edward. *The Movies In The Age Of Innocence.* Norman, 1962.

Warner, Jack L. *My First Hundred Years In Hollywood.* New York, 1965.

Warshow, Robert. *The Immediate Experience.* New York, 1964 ed.

White, W. L. "Pare Lorentz." *Scribner's* (January, 1939).

Williams, T. Harry. *Huey Long.* New York, 1969.

Williamson, A. Edmund. "Ridding Local Movies Of Gangster Films." *The American City* (September, 1931).

Wilson, Edmund. "It's Terrible! It's Ghastly! It Stinks!" *The New Republic* (July 21, 1937).

Wolfenstein, Martha, and Leites, Nathan. *Movies: A Psychological Study.* Glencoe, 1950.

Young, Stark. "Gabriel's Horn." *The New Republic* (April 19, 1933).

Zukor, Adolph. *The Public Is Never Wrong.* New York, 1953.

Index